# Aretha

# Aretha
## From These Roots

# Aretha Franklin
### and David Ritz

Villard / New York

Franklin, Aretha.
Aretha: from these roots / Aretha Franklin and David Ritz
p.    cm.
Discography: pp. 253–254
ISBN 0-375-50033-2
1. Franklin, Aretha.   2. Soul musicians—United States Biography.
I. Ritz, David.   II. Title.
ML420.F778A3   1999
782.421644'092—dc21   99-38540
[B]

Random House website address: www.atrandom.com

Printed in the United States of America on acid-free paper

98765432

First Edition

Book design by Mercedes Everett

I dedicate my book to my parents, Reverend C. L. Franklin and Barbara Siggers, who came together in love and marital bliss and out of that union came I, Aretha. They always set a positive, loving, and caring example for me. And to my children, Clarence, Eddie, Teddy, and Kecalf, who have always been loving, supportive, patient, and understanding of my professional career and commitment and who have always been there for me. And if I have reached the goal of being a good mother, and have been a guiding light and have inspired my sons to be proud, creative, independent, and productive citizens, then I have reached a priceless pinnacle in parenting.

Love, Mom

And to Erma, Vaughn, Sabrina, Christal, Thomas Garrett, Jr., and Uncle Simuel.

Love ya much

# Acknowledgments

*Aretha acknowledges . . .*

My singers: my sisters, Erma and Carolyn Franklin; my cousin Brenda Corbett; Almeda Lattimore; Evelyn Greene; Wyline Ivy; Pat Smith; Raquel Cox; Sharon Ross; Patrice Holloway; Clyde King; Gwen Guthrie; Cissy Houston, Sylvia Shemwell, Estelle Brown, Myrna Smith, and Dee Dee Warwick of the Sweet Inspirations; Darlene Love, Fanita James, and Jean King of the Blossoms; Margaret Branch; Sandra Feva; Ortheia Barnes; Billy (Always) Moore; Mae Kohn; Diane Madison; Brenda White; Marty McCall; Fonzi Thornton.

My musicians: Donald Townes, first conductor; Hindell Butts, drums; Roderick Hicks, bass; Earl Van Dyke, piano; Ray Bryant, piano; Ellis Larkins, piano; Sticks Evans, drums; Kenny Burrell, guitar; Tyree Glenn, trombone; Johnny Griffith, piano; George Davidson, drums; Charles Bowles, piano; Beans Richardson, bass; Teddy Harris, piano; Bernard Purdie, drums; Richard Tee, piano; Chuck Rainey, bass; Jerry Jemmott, bass; Horace Ott, former conductor; H. B. Barnum, present conductor; Francisco Centeno, bass; Kevin Brandon, bass; Ron Coleman, piano; Kevin Toney, piano, synthesizer; Kenny Elliott, drums; my son Teddy, of course, guitar.

My light and sound men: Clay Anderson, Tom Arco of Eight Day Sound, and Jay Barth & Co.

Any other technicians, sound and mix, who have worked with me in concert.

Anyone else whose names I've missed or forgotten, forgive me. I love you much.

A very very special thanks to Miss Kathleen Oga for her dedication to the many nights that we sat up, dictated, read, wrote, and rewrote, finishing this manuscript.

A very special thanks to Ms. Zoretha Coleman, Ms. Trudy Holliday, Ms. Janice Gersham, and Ms. Johnetta Barham, who did a smashing job in the stretch and helped me to bring this book home.

With love and appreciation, always,

Aretha

P.S. Thanks to Uly Boykin for the loan of his best executive secretaries.

*David Ritz thanks—*

Queen Aretha, for trusting me with this precious project and for the world's best vanilla-wafer banana pudding; editors David Rosenthal, Brian DeFiore, and especially the unbeatable team of Bruce Tracy and Ann Godoff; Oona Schmid; Kathleen Oga; Aaron Priest and Lisa Vance; Dick Alen; Barbara Shelley; my wonderful wife, Roberta, and fabulous daughters, Alison and Jessica; and my Detroit friends, who've been there for me from the start: Herb Boyd, Ron Locket, and Glenda Gill.

# Contents

# Contents

# Introduction

## by David Ritz

It's the day after Thanksgiving, the start of a warm winter weekend, and Aretha is rocking Detroit to its roots. She's home, she's happy, she's filled with gratitude and energy, eager to sing not only the old songs she loves so well—the red-hot R&B hits, the soaring ballads, the miraculous gospel of her childhood—but the startlingly new and expanded segment of her repertoire that includes her daring renditions of arias by Puccini. For three consecutive days in three consecutive concerts, accompanied by her own band and the venerable Detroit Symphony Orchestra, Aretha will command the stage of the city's historic Orchestra Hall and reveal, with beguiling confidence and candor, all the facets of her character that make her undisputed Queen.

She recently burned up the charts with the hip-hopped "A Rose Is Still a Rose," her biggest record in twenty years. Substituting for Luciano Pavarotti at the last minute, she defied the gods of reason by infusing "Nessun dorma" with deep soul, convincing a worldwide live audience of a billion Grammy viewers that no melodic music was beyond her reach. On a VH1 special entitled "Divas Live," the other divas disappeared; the Queen and Queen alone ruled the night.

The Queen has been on a roll, and it was in the midst of this extraordinary streak that she and I sat down in the living room of her Detroit home and spoke of her life. We met over a period spanning four years. Our conversations were probing. The process was new for Aretha, who had never before been interviewed at such length. The process was also new for me, who had never before interviewed a Queen. The Queen on stage, though, was one thing—regal, even glorious—while the Queen in the living room was quite another.

The Queen in the living room was as real as rain, a woman who spoke eloquently but bluntly. Among her photographs and plants, her pots and pans, her walls of awards, her stacks of videos on everything from learning French to the latest Donna Karan collection, Aretha is comfortable. Aretha loves her home. She's fond of quoting Roseanne on being a "domestic goddess." She loves being surrounded by friends, family, and the people she most closely trusts—those with whom she has worked and lived longest. In this cozy atmosphere, the house filled with familiar kitchen fragrances, she finds it only natural, even easy, to return to memories of her past.

For well over thirty years, journalists have often given us an impression of an Aretha they do not know. They've analyzed and mythologized, speculated and flat-out invented a character who bears little resemblance to the real Aretha, the Aretha sitting in the living room telling you about her father, her fond remembrances of Sam Cooke, her passion for roller skating, her days playing teenybop hops one night and sophisticated supper clubs the next, her feelings about other divas and other days when disco pulled the rug from under the soul stars and life was a challenge.

Writing this book with Aretha was a challenge, a great challenge, because Aretha insisted that all the thoughts and all the words be absolutely true to her heart. She was a careful and conscientious collaborator, checking every line against the sincerity of her soul. That's how she sings. That's how she is. More than anything, the process of working with Aretha took me back to my first book, the autobiography I wrote with Ray Charles. Like Ray, Aretha is uncompromisingly individual, firmly in command of her life, her art, and her career. There is no one like her. Like Ray, her music is the product of the black church; and also like Ray, her music has crossed over genre after genre to include anything she chooses to sing. While embracing new genres, she also has the uncanny ability to change those genres, infusing them with a spirit—the spirit in the dark—that has a way of lighting up the world.

There's no need to describe the Aretha I encountered in the living room, because her words do that for her. As she herself declares, she is a people person. And the person she wants to reach, the person she wants to understand what she has been through and who she is, is you.

In this book, which she has waited a lifetime to write, Aretha speaks for herself.

# Aretha

# *Precious Memories*

⌒

Three months after the attack on Pearl Harbor, while the world was ablaze in war, I made my debut. I was born Aretha Louise Franklin on March 25, in Memphis, Tennessee, named after my father's two sisters, Aretha and Louise.

My father, Reverend Clarence LaVaughn Franklin, and mother, Barbara V. Siggers, were known and respected in the African American church communities of Mississippi and Tennessee and the surrounding religious circuit. And subsequently, my parents had five children together—my sister Erma, brother Vaughn and brother Cecil, me, and my baby sister, Carolyn. We're all approximately two years apart.

My mother was a superb singer, her voice clear and distinctive. She also played piano in traditional gospel style. She was a nurse's aide, which is why I considered being a nurse at a young age. At Christmas she would give my sister Carolyn and me little play nurses' kits with stethoscopes, candy pills, and Band-Aids. We loved the candy pills, similar to Tic-Tacs. Carolyn and I would give each other checkups and pretend to listen to our hearts and lungs with the stethoscopes. Mom also gave us beautiful black dolls that were tucked in storm coats that we just loved, and the colors of the storm coats were blue and green. Eventually all our dolls were semibald. What happened to the hair? We combed and styled it out.

My parents met in Shelby, Mississippi. As a young preacher, Daddy arrived there from Sunflower County in the Delta, where he had picked cotton and worked the life of a sharecropper. Daddy always said he dreamed of—and always knew there was—a better way beyond the cotton fields.

On occasion he recalled how, from time to time, he would jump down off the old mule and start preaching. Later on he asked my grandmother if he could work on the migrant workers' trucks heading north. She agreed, and he almost had a serious accident as two trucks hinged together. He jumped out of the way just in time.

My grandmother, whom we called Big Mama, had worked the fields herself and told us stories of those difficult days. No matter how much cotton you picked, you always owed the man. Daddy had to walk ten or fifteen miles to school. But he did it, he found education and set his sights on bettering himself. He and my mother moved to Memphis, where he pastored two churches.

It was also in Memphis that Daddy attended LeMoyne College, studying sociology and English literature. At LeMoyne he challenged his fundamentalist upbringing and welcomed more liberal ways of viewing the Bible. He took those ways to Buffalo, New York, where he pastored the Friendship Baptist Church and my mom served as choir director and pianist.

When I was two we moved from Buffalo to Detroit, a city Daddy viewed as dynamic. Those were the years when Ford was promising all workers five dollars a day out at the plant in River

Rouge. Detroit was on the move. Replacing Reverend Horatio Coleman, Daddy became pastor of the New Bethel Baptist Church, which would eventually locate at 4210 Hastings Street.

With help from Household Finance, a loan agency, he supplemented his income from church. I recall seeing a book of food stamps once, though I don't know if he ever used them. However he managed, he made a comfortable and secure home for us.

My parents separated when I was six. Despite the fact that it has been written innumerable times, it is an absolute lie that my mother abandoned us. In no way, shape, form, or fashion did our mother desert us. She was extremely responsible, loving, and caring. She simply moved with Vaughn back to Buffalo, where she lived with her parents, Clara and Reverend Wafford. My parents decided we would stay with my dad, who was in a better position to care for us on a daily basis. And he did. Mom couldn't afford to raise five children on a nurse's aide's salary. However, she communicated with us by phone and regular visits. She never lost sight of her children or her parenting responsibilities—and her visits continued regularly. She sent us beautiful gifts, and we traveled to Buffalo to spend the summers with her yearly.

In those days adults didn't discuss their affairs with children. Of course, I wondered why my parents had separated, and I wanted them to stay together; small children, though, were respectful of adult matters. My parents were mindful not to speak harsh words in our presence; they had the wisdom to know that children need a strong, positive, and united image of both mother and father.

I loved those summer visits. Mom lived in a duplex on Lythe Street in Cold Springs, a beautiful neighborhood in Buffalo. In the late forties and early fifties, the area was middle-class black, characterized by good-sized and well-maintained homes, two-story structures of brick and wood. I remember Buffalo as a city of wide boulevards and towering trees that lightly shaded the streets where we played.

Mom's home was beautifully decorated with blue-and-silver velvet chairs and couches, an upright piano in the back room, and family pictures everywhere. My mother's family in the area were Uncles Mims, Simuel, Cecil, Bo, and Reginald; Aunts Izora and Knobbie and Rubella; and one of my first cousins, Faye, whose picture I always admired. She was a pretty girl who looked very official in her WAC uniform.

My brother Vaughn was a track star at Masten High School and had beautiful medals to prove it. When we were small children, Vaughn also took us up to the stadium, where we swam in the public pool. We spent hours riding our bikes, and once I recall passing a nightclub where folks were lined up for blocks. Inside B. B. King was playing loud enough for us to hear, the sound of his guitar spilling out onto the sidewalk. I stood there for a while with my bike and listened before riding away.

I was registered to attend Public School Number 8 in Buffalo and attended for a short while.

My mom was disciplined at her nursing profession. She worked at Buffalo General Hospital. When my sisters, brother, and I were with her, we were always happy. But because her folks' house had only two bedrooms, she arranged for us to stay in the home next door, with Mr. and Mrs. Dan Pitman. Mrs. Pitman introduced me to the fine art of crocheting, showing me her beautiful tablecloths, hankies, bedspreads, and doilies. I took to the craft right away. She was my first crocheting instructor, and to this day I enjoy crocheting various items for family and friends; I like maneuvering subtle pumpkin and pineapple stitches. As I crochet, I often think of those days in Buffalo and Mr. and Mrs. Pitman.

Mother's friend, Trustee Young, was a jovial and good man who lived on Waverly Street, where I rode my bike up and down the rolling hills until dusk. Trustee also occasionally took us out riding in his car. During one such ride, Mother was seated next to Trustee with Carolyn on her lap. We hadn't been driving long when suddenly *bang!* Someone smashed into the back of our car, violently throwing us forward. No one was really hurt, but I heard Trustee say that if Mom hadn't been holding Carolyn, she would have gone through the windshield. Thank God for my mother's firm grip.

Mom had neighbors called the Blasingames, whose daughter Charlotte was a friend of mine. But it was all about her brother Gordon. Gordon was my first teenybop crush. He was older and didn't even know I existed. I'd sit on the steps of Mrs. Pitman's porch just to catch a glimpse of him coming or going. When he made an appearance, I would silently swoon. And my heart did extra palpitations. *Ooooooooooooooooh!*

Days flew by, and summer passed too quickly. Charlotte, Gordon, my secret love, and other neighborhood children—Christine, Buddy, and Yvonne—all lived at the end of Lythe Street. Mr. Cohen's grocery store had the biggest dill pickles, and Buffalo's Texas Red Hots (hot dogs) were covered with the best chili in America. I never wanted summer to end. Riding home, I cherished the memories of all the summer surprises and some unknown neighborhood boy who would come out at midnight and stand in the middle of Lythe Street, where, at the top of his voice, he sang the words "Hurry home, come home." I loved it and could count on him the same time every night, saying to myself as I turned over in bed, drifting off to sleep, *Who is that crazy boy?*

# Tenderheaded

By the time I was eight, the fifties had officially begun. Korea was heating up as a war zone, while President Harry Truman rolled back the prices on new cars. Naturally I knew none of this. I was busy in my own little world watching TV—Howdy Doody, Sid Caesar and Imogene Coca, and the *Texaco Star Theatre* were my favorites. I loved traveling the Queen's Highway between Detroit and Buffalo. Daddy did a wonderful job in making us feel secure and setting a very strong and positive example. I was a daddy's girl mainly because of my parents' separation, but I respected and loved both Mother and Father.

We lived in the church parish, a large six-bedroom house on Boston Boulevard, on the North End of the city. Our home was right at the corner of Oakland, the central thoroughfare, which split the neighborhood into various economic classes. Our street was characterized by manicured lawns and lovely landscaping. An island in the middle of the boulevard was planted with shrubs and small trees. Charles Diggs, Sr., a black congressman, lived on the corner down the block; on another corner was Dr. Harold Stitts, a prominent physician.

Inside, our home was tastefully appointed. The living room was decorated with beautiful drapes of purple satin with big flowers tone on tone and plush green carpeting, an elaborate Emerson TV, and a grand piano by the window. I loved looking out at the passing traffic and watching people on the street as I doodled at the piano. I am a people person.

Our backyard was filled with fruit trees. Pears, plums, crab apples, and apples bore lush, lovely blossoms in spring and summer. During harsh winters, snowdrifts would pile high and sometimes, to our delight, school was canceled.

Saturday nights were warm and wonderful. The kitchen was filled with the aroma of baked ham, fried corn, and homemade rolls. Lola Moore, Daddy's friend, was fashionable, fun, and a dynamite cook. After the best Saturday night dinner, my brother Vaughn would give us our Saturday night baths. Then Lola would sit me, Carolyn, and Erma in the big overstuffed chair planted in the middle of the kitchen by the stove, and, holding the strands at the base of my head, slowly comb through my hair to create Shirley Temple curls. Lola tried to be gentle, but it hurt all the same. I was tenderheaded, and although I wasn't a crying child, tears welled up in my eyes every time.

Our household was superactive. Music was always in the air. We had two pianos. Erma might be practicing "Flight of the Bumble Bee" on our old upright; Erma was a virtuoso with that piece—she played it perfectly or her teacher, Mr. Shelby, would rap her fingers with his pencils. I might be running up and down the stairs, jumping four or five at a time, dashing in and out of the house. The piano, the radio, the record player might all be going at once. When my piano teacher came to the house, I would hide behind the coats in the back of the closet because I thought her exercises far too elementary; I wanted to skip to the intermediate material. It never occurred to me to complain to my dad that I didn't want lessons. I thought they were mandatory, and complaining wouldn't have done me any good. I wanted to run before I could walk.

Today I wish I had learned to sight-read, and I will, which is the reason I'm enrolling at the Juilliard School of Music, the most prestigious institution of its kind in the country. On the other hand, playing by ear, as I've done throughout my life, has allowed me to develop a rather personal and signature style, which I treasure and would not give up for anything or anyone.

One afternoon when I came home from school, I heard an especially brilliant style of music. Seated behind our grand piano was a heavyset man, a cigarette dangling from his mouth. The cigarette ash was incredibly long, yet it never fell as the pianist tilted his head to avoid the smoke floating into his eyes. His playing caught my ear. I was too young, however, to fully appreciate his genius. When my father introduced him as his friend Art Tatum, the name made no particular impression on me. Only later would I realize that I had met in our very living room the man most musicians consider the world's greatest jazz pianist. I also had great respect for the piano stylings of Nat "King" Cole, whom I often heard in our home as well. I loved his "Mona Lisa" and "Too Young."

For a while my dad's mother, Big Mama, lived with us. She was a devout Christian—and a great comedian. Her husband, Big Papa, was an invalid, confined to their bedroom just off the upstairs back porch. A stroke had impaired his speech and right side. He was a kind man, and I loved lighting his pipe for him. I'd pack the tobacco, strike the match, and draw strongly before handing him the pipe. It was my first little experience smoking. You couldn't really call it smoking, though; I hadn't picked up the habit—yet. I would sit there and talk to Big Papa, and he would gesture for whatever he wanted. I still remember a picture that hung in their room—a beautiful black angel adorned in a violet velvet robe.

On some nights after I had gone to bed, out of the darkness I'd hear a knock on the door and Daddy saying, "Ree, come on downstairs. I'd like you to play and sing a couple of things."

The first few times this happened, I was excited and flattered, but thereafter less so. I was sleepy and didn't want to drag myself out of bed. But I was an obedient daughter and did what Daddy asked. Following him downstairs, I heard people talking and laughing in the living room. There was a small gathering of his friends.

I slid onto the piano bench and played "Canadian Sunset," the instrumental version by Eddie Heywood I had heard on the radio. This was the number that had let Daddy know I had talent. Strictly by ear, I could copy Heywood's interpretation note for note. Then Daddy liked me to sing songs like "I Wish I Didn't Love You So" and "Don't Get Around Much Anymore." At a young age I had a strong voice. When I was all through with my minirecital, everyone applauded. They were pleased and Daddy was proud.

On Sunday mornings Lola combed out our hair so that our Shirley Temple curls were extra-bouncy. After breakfast Daddy, my sisters, my brother, Lola, and I all piled into the car as we headed for church. I remember the route: from the North End to the East Side, down Oakland to Bethune to Brush, past Mr. Dixon's barbershop—Jeff Dixon was one of Daddy's deacons and a charter member of New Bethel—to Forest to Hastings to Willis. The corner of Hastings and Willis, 4210 Hastings. The New Bethel Baptist Church.

Sometimes I would leave our church and go across the street to the little storefront Holiness Church, where they were shouting and praising His name so strong that I was drawn inside to enjoy the gospel.

Our church was a beautiful modern edifice of blond bricks. Graceful stained-glass windows, reflecting the morning sun, depicted scenes of Jesus and the disciples. Red carpet and blond wood chairs decorated the pulpit. The outer lobby was a walled-in picture window, allowing you to see into the splendid sanctuary. Compared with our first building, which was old and dark, this one was bright and inspiring. It was my dad's leadership, foresight, and initiative, along with the church's committed membership—and the fund-raising efforts of people like Sylvia Penn, Thomas Shelby, Eliza Butler, and others—that built the new structure.

Daddy was a handsome man who stood over six feet tall. His manner was friendly, humanitarian, and down-to-earth. He could speak the language of the intellectual and the wise theologian. He was also a trendsetter and pioneer. In those days he was the first African American minister on radio and also among the first black preachers to travel the country because of his recorded sermons. He took great pride in his appearance and never dressed in drab colors. He was style and class at its best. He bought his tailored custom suits from Ben and Harry Koskins of Koskins Clothiers in downtown Detroit. His hair was conservatively processed with a few finger waves, the work of Benny Mullins, his longtime barber. He was supersharp and what Sylvia Penn used to call stinky sharp, Sylvia being an old charter member of the church and chaperone to us girls on numerous occasions. (Sometimes Sylvia's imagination ran away with her when she took us shopping with Daddy's money—but more on that later. I liked Sylvia a lot. She was a work of art.)

Some called Daddy the High Priest of Soul Preaching. Some

called him Reverend. His closest friends called him C.L., and the more fly parishioners referred to him as the Black Prince. But the name he liked most was Rabbi, which was also coined by Sylvia. Daddy liked being called Rabbi because, in addition to his work as a preacher, he was a teacher and scholar. He loved his theology classes and was a living example of his own creed that said you're never too old to learn. He continued his education well after college with extension courses and religious teachings as both student and teacher with his weekly classes with other minister friends in the city, like Reverends Charles Adams, Lee Jackson, Reuben Gayton, David Hudson, and O'Neil Swanson, Sr.

When I was nine or ten, I sang my first solo in church. I had been performing with the junior choir for a while, but this was special. We sang from the floor, directly behind the pianist. Looking out at the congregation, I saw some fifteen hundred people worshipping.

Buddy Upshaw, a terrific pianist, was our choir director. With the choir behind me, we would rock the church. I sang "Jesus Be a Fence Around Me," a song I first heard by Sam Cooke and the Soul Stirrers. Big Mama was right there in her favorite seat, nodding her approval and encouraging me with all the power and passion of her faith. Big Mama would often be overcome with the gospel. She'd start shouting and moving and turning over three or four huge flower arrangements until she'd have to be restrained. My Uncle Benny, an usher, sometimes did the restraining along with others who would complain afterward that Aunt Rachel—that's Big Mama—had scuffed up their shoes again.

I always had my grandmother's unrestrained support as she shouted, "Sing out, Aretha!" or "Oh, yes!" When Daddy spoke, she'd cry, "You're mighty right!" and the deacons and trustees would have to stop her as she headed for her son, shouting and crying with the spirit while remembering the hard times that she and my Aunt Louise had come through in Mississippi—the cotton fields, the sharecropping.

When Daddy was preaching, the parishioners would shout "Amen" and echo many of the things he was saying. If at any time it got quiet, he would stop and say, "Wake up that lady sitting next to you!" The church would crack up. Or he would say, "Are you praying with me?" or "Listen, if you please."

When he would get into what I call high or third gear, it was called whooping. Later Harry Belafonte called Daddy a super-whooper, a description that made me smile. I second that emotion. It is also commonly called a squall. Whooping is a powerful and highly rhythmic way of preaching in which words take the form of song—half speech, half melody. Reverend Jesse Jackson, whose ordination sermon was delivered by Daddy, said, "C. L. Franklin was the most imitated soul preacher in history, a combination of soul and science and substance and sweetness."

Daddy got into a deep groove when the message was moving him. He'd lay down his glasses and carry on fervently. Everyone would be on their feet, testifying and praising the Lord. The whole church would be up and shouting, "Go ahead!" and "Yes, sir!" I can hear it as clearly as if it were yesterday on the soundtrack of my memory.

After his sermon Daddy might sing a hymn, "Father, I Stretch My Hands to Thee," which was his favorite, or "Old Ship of Zion." His singing voice was as big, warm, and soulful as his preaching voice. I know he could have been a major vocalist and star had he chosen to. Instead, he exemplified his Christian beliefs every day. He had a higher calling.

While Daddy spoke and sang, sometimes my mind was on the sermon and what he was saying. If I had not had breakfast, though,

I was really looking forward to the after-church dinner. We began at 11:00 A.M., so by 3:00 P.M. I would be terrifically hungry. Making matters worse were the aromas floating from the church kitchen across the street. I could smell the chicken frying in those huge black cast-iron skillets; I could taste the baked macaroni and cheese and ham hocks and candied sweet potatoes swimming in butter and cinnamon, the homemade ice cream hand-stirred by the older sisters in the church. I'd eat so much homemade ice cream I'd actually have a headache by the time I finished.

# Other Sundays,
# Other Voices

When the Ward Singers came to Detroit for the first time, I was sitting on the edge of my seat.

I had never heard a voice like Clara Ward's—and still haven't. I was only a small child, but after hearing Clara—and later Reverend James Cleveland—there was no question in my mind that one day I would be a singer. The other Ward Singers were super too, virtuosos who would live on as legends of gospel: Marion Williams, who became an international star and was featured in *Black Nativity*, which enjoyed a most successful Broadway run; Henrietta Waddy, whose version of "Get Back Jordan" was the greatest; Frances Steadman; and Kitty Parham, who turned out to be as avid a Sam Cooke fan as I was.

The Wards had visual as well as vocal flair. At a time when gospel groups wore robes, the Wards wore gowns. They loved fashion and found nothing inconsistent between a flashy presentation and passionate love of God. The two worked together. They loved sequins, bouffant hairstyles, and chignons. Clara used to have triple chignons (balls) and was noted for wearing some of the world's most beautiful gowns. As legend has it, one Sunday when Clara was performing she became so emotionally caught up in the spirit that two of the balls fell off. Not to worry. Clara just reached down with one hand, picked up the balls, and put them on top of the piano without missing a beat.

Daddy and Clara were great friends. They both were pioneers. The Wards integrated Las Vegas in the early days; they were the first black female gospel group to perform in the showrooms, namely the Frontier Hotel. Although they did not stay in the hotel, they did integrate the showroom. That was typical of Clara and Daddy. They were broad-minded in their attitudes and absolutely subscribed to the biblical mandate that the gospel be spread all over the world. Clara made a joyful noise wherever she went.

The Wards were singing evangelists. Founded and managed by their mother, Miss Gertrude Ward, they took gospel from country churches to New York nightclubs and European concert halls. Everyone loved Clara, from her Hollywood friends like Mitzi Gaynor and Dinah Shore to young, aspiring gospel singers like me. Clara ruled nationally as well as in her hometown of Philadelphia, where other young girls like Patti LaBelle surely noted her wide-brimmed hats and fabulous style. Even though Patti developed an original and passionate styling of her own, I believe she appreciated Clara.

I was so excited when, after a Ward concert at the Church of Our Prayer, a Detroit sanctuary led by Reverend James Lofton, Clara invited me to join her in the lobby for dinner. That's where I got my first lesson in eating fried chicken. I observed how she picked up a chicken leg and, instead of devouring it—like I would have—handled it very delicately. Extending her pinkie, she took small, ladylike bites. In contrast, I had more of a common grip.

As I look back, Clara's influence on me seems much like the influence I've had on Natalie Cole and Whitney Houston, both of whom I appreciate and enjoy. Whitney, whom I've always called Nippy, has grown beautifully since her early work and developed into a stylist in her own right.

The style of gospel singing exemplified by Clara Ward became the great musical influence of my early childhood. Later I learned that the fifties, the main decade of my childhood, was considered the Golden Age of Gospel. All the great gospel luminaries came to Detroit, and many to my dad's church. Others, like the Allegro Trio, a first-rate group, came out of our own choir. New Bethel was a beacon of good-news gospel power as well as an example of what a church should be: every Sunday for over thirty years my father helped indigent families get back on their feet. He never missed a Sunday without soliciting donations on behalf of needy people in our congregation who could not afford food or rent. This was something he never forgot.

My early introduction to classical music involved my sister Erma and Sylvia Burston, Smokey Robinson's niece, in our home on Boston Boulevard. I was seven or eight. We were all sitting on the floor in front of the big antique radio, and Sylvia and Erma, both older than I, were listening to Mario Lanza. Sylvia was so touched, with her ear pressed against the speakers of the radio, she began to cry. For the life of me, I could not understand why she was crying to Mario Lanza, since we didn't listen to classical artists anyway. I thought it was funny; every time I'd think about it, I'd start laughing. Only later, as a teenager, did I recognize her sensitivity to the music and how touching it was for her.

Rhythm and blues was also a strong part of my life. After coming in from school and putting down my books, I'd hear deejays like Rocking with Leroy blasting Ruth Brown or LaVern Baker.

Or I'd stretch out on the floor in front of the big radio and listen to Senator Bristol Bryant, the gospel deejay of the time, who would play my favorites—the Caravans (Albertina Walker, Inez Andrews, Delores Washington, Dorothy Norwood, and Cassietta George), the Sensational Nightingales, the Dixie Hummingbirds, and the Swan Silvertones. I loved them all. Gospel nourished my soul.

Remember, too, this was a time of high optimism in Detroit. The music reflected that optimism, the belief that things were getting better for black folks. You had a huge migration from the South; hundreds of thousands of black Americans, my dad and grandmother among them, had traveled north to the Motor City—and to Chicago, Pittsburgh, Cleveland, and New York—in search of a better life for themselves and their families.

We also heard about the race riots in Detroit's past. Our next-door neighbors, Richard Ross and the Ross family, our first friends in the neighborhood, told such tales. Richard took delight in these dramatic stories, holding our attention for hours.

In 1952, President Truman ordered seizure of the steel mills to avert a strike by the steelworkers. That had to be the talk of the town, especially when the Supreme Court overruled him two months later and the workers went on strike. Labor disputes were always big news in the city of my childhood. Generally, though, it was a time of prosperity. Detroit was a hardworking, socially conscious city just hitting its stride. At New Bethel Baptist Church, Daddy preached self-pride. Anticipating a movement that wouldn't arrive for another decade, Daddy argued against stereotypes of the past.

"We are black," he said from the pulpit, "not because we are cursed, for blackness is not a curse; it is a curse only if you think so, and it's not really a curse then; it's just the way you think. All colors are beautiful in the sight of God. The only reason why you entertain a thought like that is because you have been culturally conditioned by some white people to think that way, and they conditioned you that way because they used this as a means to an end, to give you a feeling of inferiority, and to then take advantage of you, socially, economically, and politically."

Pride was something Daddy gave us in abundance. I never felt inferior or less than. I was blessed to grow up in an environment where self-worth was underscored. Later, as a civil rights activist and close colleague of Dr. Martin Luther King, Jr., my father was instrumental in social betterment. He fought against discrimination. He fought the good fight. His pulpit was a platform for many local and national speakers, including Dr. Adam Clayton Powell, Sr., Dr. Caesar Clarke, Dr. King, Reverend Jesse Jackson, and many local politicians running for office.

It happened when I was ten. Daddy called all of us—me, Erma, Carolyn, and Cecil—into the kitchen. As he sat at the end of the sink, which resembled a sideboard, he said it plainly and solemnly. Our mother had suffered a fatal heart attack.

I just stood there, stunned.

I cannot describe the pain, nor will I try. Pain is sometimes a private matter, and the pain of small children losing their mother defies description.

Daddy couldn't have been more understanding. Earlier he had recorded a song called "Your Mother Loves Her Children." As I listened to it, I felt he had written it for us.

We went to Buffalo for the funeral, and afterward, for a long, long time, I sat on the curb on Lythe Street across from my mother's house. Just sat there in the sun and thought of my mom and the many times we spent together. Sat there in tears and kept thinking of her. It helped make me feel a little better. I recalled lovely afternoons, after she returned home from work, when I would be standing on the porch to greet her. And then she, Carolyn, and I would sit in the rocking chair, and she'd talk to us softly of better things to come.

# Mother's Day

The church gave me comfort. Like my father, the church always gave me a special kind of love.

I remember Mother's Day, when the church mothers sat in the first row. I loved the beautiful hats that the ladies wore with such pride. Big Mama and the church mothers were the backbone of New Bethel. We also had other colorful personalities such as Thomas H. Shelby, the senior pianist and choir director; Lucille Marshal, who was the church announcer for the broadcast; Eliza Butler and Harry Kincaid, Sr., charter members of the church; and Lucy Branch, the mother of Margaret, one of my current background singers. Lucy was a soloist who traveled with my dad for his out-of-town services.

The church nurses carried smelling salts to revive worshippers who were overcome to the point of fainting by the spirit and/or Daddy's sermons. Before speaking, Daddy might sing a hymn like "I Love the Lord, He Heard Me Cry." And when the hymn was sung, he would take his text. His manner was clear, precise, and sin-

cere. He spoke of Hannah. "Hannah," said Daddy, "was the ideal mother."

He spoke of modern marriage and modern motherhood. "There are those who do not believe in divorce," he explained, "based on the idea 'Let that which God has joined together, let no man put asunder.' But you can't tell me that all the folk who are married today, God joined them together!" He had the congregation laughing, he had the congregation listening to his thoughts that motherhood is a divine duty and responsibility, that mothers must mold their children during their "impressionable years."

Then he would stop and ask, "Are you praying with me?

"Pardon me for being personal." He paused to reflect. "But I learned to pray from my mother. She was a praying mother. And her faith in God was contagious for me."

I saw Big Mama affirming his words, nodding. "Oh, yes!"

"Well," said Daddy, "Hannah's faith is contagious. She desired to be a mother. Didn't go to the priests with her desire, but went directly to God. I don't believe you know what I'm talking about. I said, *Hannah was a praying mother.* And my mother is a praying mother. I must become personal again. These things live with you. One night I was graduating from fifth or sixth grade, and I had to give a little speech, but I spoke so low the audience couldn't hear me. My mother looked at me in a certain way. I knew I was in for it. That night she said, 'When I get through with you, next time you get up to speak, you are going to speak.' And I've been speaking ever since. And I mean speaking where folk can hear me. Modern psychologists might not recommend Aunt Rachel's approach, but it worked on me."

The church was laughing again; the church loved the way Daddy brought home the lesson. I thought how Big Mama still applied that lesson to us when we did things we had no business doing. She would send us out to break off the biggest switch on the tree and bring it back to her. If it was too small, we had to go back and get another. Big Mama would save up our whippings and give us two or three in one session. Just when we thought we had gotten away with it, she would remind us and talk to us for a long, long time before raising the switch. And she'd ask, "Now are you going to do that again?" And we'd say, "No, ma'am, we're not going to do that again." We were sure we had avoided a whipping. *Wrong!* Before we could move away, *Whap!* She was holding on to you as she worked her way around you. I learned to perfect a high-jumping technique at whipping time, and many times I jumped so high the switch missed me. But sometimes Big Mama would catch me on the downstroke. Big Mama was something else.

Daddy was still sermonizing, speaking on parent-child relationships, moving into the whooping stage:

> "I believe it's a wonderful thing
>   to have a son or a daughter
>   to say to you, 'Mother, I still love you,
>   for you stood by me
>   and
>   I appreciate all the things
>   that you did for me
>   Oh Lord
>   and
>   in my coming up maybe
>   I acted like I didn't appreciate it
>   but it was only because I didn't understand you then
>   but now I know
>   yes, I do'
>   Holy God

From my own experience I can say
those brought up properly still hold on to it
and look back on their parents with
reverence and respect
Pray with me if you please
They may run wild
They may go astray
But they will come home
To Mother, oh yes they will."

He was in the stretch and all the way up, reaching the hearts of everyone—mothers and fathers, daughters and sons—when he concluded with a story about a daughter who goes astray, abandons her mother, only to wind up sick in a distant city, where she finally finds the strength to call for her mother to come and tend to her wasted body and injured soul. Mother comes and daughter is healed.

"Thank God for my mother," said Daddy. "Thank God for my mother, who told me the Lord is a door when every other door is closed."

Big Mama had an unshakable faith in God. And a lighthearted humor. For instance, you'd never catch Big Mama dancing, but if certain records with a good beat were playing, you might see her doing a little shuffle once in a blue moon with a fixed expression on her face that would crack me up. There was a period when she lived on Hawthorne Avenue in Highland Park with my cousin Brenda, Aunt Louise's daughter. When Aunt Louise died of cancer, Big Mama took over and raised Brenda.

I recall all of the housekeepers hired by Daddy to care for us.

Mrs. Howard was the first. She was a disciplinarian and a cook who could teach Julia Child a trick or two. Mrs. Howard introduced us to corned beef and cabbage and mountain oysters. Later, when I found out what mountain oysters really were—bull testicles—I nearly keeled over. We got a kick out of the Best sisters, Ersterlen and Geneva. These ladies were superfly and daring, one shocking platinum, the other bold blond. I loved their hair and their flair. I also remember Amelia and Mrs. Hopkins, our favorite, who serves on the Usher Board of New Bethel to this day.

Sylvia, our housekeeper Katherine, and Big Mama taught me how to cook. And now I'm good and mean with the pots. These were the serious soul sisters with those big black cast-iron skillets and huge vats of ham hocks and fresh green beans, fried corn, white potatoes and candied sweet potatoes, pigs' feet, pineapple upside-down cakes, and all those scrumptious delicacies. Sometimes after church Daddy would let us go home with Mrs. Crayton, who taught me to make homemade ice cream; I'd be stirring those wooden spoons forever and sampling little tastes as I went along, asking every ten minutes or so, "Is it ready now?"

Sylvia Penn made a mean meat loaf and mixed greens, which I added to my repertoire. And Lola, Daddy's lady friend, was like a second mom. We would also visit Lola and her family in Chicago during later summers. We loved Lola. She was one of the few beautiful role models for us girls. She had a great sense of humor and was caring and real in the absence and loss of our mother. Lola actually moved in and lived with us for a while. She came closer to marrying Daddy than anyone else. Officially or unofficially, some people don't need the paper. Lola did lots of canning, preserving jars of crab apples and pears and peaches and tasty jellies and jams that sat perfectly on the side of the dinner plate. This is the style I love—cooking the old-fashioned way, from scratch.

The day Lola left was sad. It happened after she had lived with us for several years. When the cab came to pick her up, we were all crying—Lola included, and especially Cecil. We understood she had to go, but Cecil couldn't let go. I can still see him holding on to the cab door, running beside the cab, doing everything in his power to keep Lola from catching her train. We all wished Lola could have stayed. But Daddy's personal affairs were not our business, and we knew not to question him.

Daddy was a minister, and he was also a man. Some women pursued him aggressively night and day, and in the front row sitting rather high. One actually showed up at the house with a suitcase. He wasn't there at the time, but the woman talked Carolyn into letting her in. When I became aware of it, the lady was at the top of the staircase as I was coming into the hallway. Carolyn snapped into action. She grabbed a kitchen knife—remember, she was just a little girl—ran up the steps, jumped in front of the woman, and backed her down the stairs and out of the house. With her quick strategy, Carolyn really shocked me that day. Carolyn had chutzpah and heart.

My older sister, Erma, had and has a very grand side to her. Daddy used to call her Madam Queen. Much later, coming out of Clark College in Atlanta, Georgia, she learned to spar intellectually. She loved challenging Daddy. She could be loving and caring or cool and aloof. It depended on which fish was swimming what way. As a Pisces, Erma could be swimming upstream or down.

My brother Cecil was most beautiful, intelligent, cool, and sensitive. He liked modern jazz, and he particularly liked Sarah Vaughan; *In the Land of Hi-Fi* was one of his favorite albums. He loved listening to Sarah while doing his homework, being a student at Northern High School and later Morehouse College in Atlanta, where he graduated cum laude. *In the Land of Hi-Fi* and Cecil still play on the soundtrack of my childhood. At age ten I also had an early taste of jazz with Charlie Parker's "My Little Suede Shoes," a favorite along with cuts by Max Roach and Clifford Brown.

I told you that Carolyn had lots of spunk. One of the funniest stories about Carolyn is when Sylvia Penn took us shopping in the early fifties to Demery's, an upscale department store on Woodward and Milwaukee. Daddy would give Sylvia a set sum of money to buy us each a complete outfit. I presumed that Sylvia was honest and would do exactly as my dad had instructed. I'm not saying that she wasn't, but Carolyn didn't presume as much. At the tender age of eight, Carolyn would keep her own little record of what Sylvia was spending. Well, when Sylvia was ready to leave, Carolyn wasn't; she and Sylvia had a loud knock-down-drag-out in the middle of Demery's, with Carolyn insisting that all her money had not been spent on her. Carolyn was very aware and demanded an accounting of everything before she would leave the store.

I attended Alger Elementary School, where my teacher, Ida B. Hooper, taught me much about perseverance. Later I went to Hutchins Junior High, where my grades were good. Generally I liked most of my instructors. Miss Adamo was one teacher who worshipped Bishop Fulton Sheen, the television clergyman. She tried to bring prayer into the classroom in those days. I recall being put out of her class for being too outspoken about prayer in the classroom. I fondly recall other teachers—Miss Irene Morgan, Miss Julia Preer, Miss Sanford, Miss Gwendolyne Hogue (my first art teacher), Miss Merriweather, Miss Frankie Davis (our gym instructor and one of my favorites); and Miss Betty Lackey, former president of the Detroit Branch of the NAACP—God rest her soul.

I learned harmony in the third grade in the glee club. We did a unique version of "The Star-Spangled Banner." I also wanted to join the band but applied too late to get the instrument of my choice. For a while I played flute. My teacher had me put my name on the instrument with tape, and I found the flute rather delightful. I wound up with a tuba, however, because everything else was taken; I blew one note here and one note there.

Outside of school my friends were Richard Ross and his half sister, Lenore, who had a wild sense of humor, and Helen Leberrie and the Leberrie family. Richard's house was also the scene of an important and basic discovery of mine—a bacon, lettuce, and tomato sandwich. Lenore and I had several fun nights just making sandwiches with the toaster, the latest invention. I remember Helen and me standing before the mirror, arguing—as silly as it sounds—about whose set of teeth was more beautiful.

The Hollys were also close friends. They were a loving family of six children who were incredibly generous. Mrs. Holly made the best pot of chicken and dumplings you've ever tasted.

From my bedroom across the way, I observed several extrafine men who roomed at the Rosses'. I was far too young to be interested in these older guys. But they did catch my eye momentarily—and then my shade came down fast.

I also recall Gloreyce and Laureyce, the twins who lived on Oakland, who wore the cutest little sunsuits. I wanted a sunsuit like theirs, and finally Daddy bought me several. On our street proper, there weren't many girls, so I wound up playing with the boys. You could say I was a tomboy then. I could run and skip and climb trees with the best of them; I could jump out of trees fourteen and fifteen feet off the ground after climbing as high as I wanted to. Mr. Ross set up a little contest to see who could run fastest and jump highest. I believe he was trying to see if any of us had Olympic potential. I won most of the races as well as the high jumping. The hurdles, though, came tumbling down when he put them too high.

I reminisce about summers past—playing in the little park in front of our home. One balmy evening I had a significant feminine awakening. Someone threw a basketball that hit me smack-dab in the chest. I cried loud enough to be heard a mile away. I was through playing for the day, and my T-shirt-free days were over.

"Aretha," said Big Mama, "it's time for your first bra. You're growing up."

⁘

When Daddy went out of town on business, he left us with responsible housekeepers and my grandmother. One of those adults, a colleague called Reverend Gayton, who was his houseguest at the time, didn't turn out so responsible. During the time Daddy was gone, Reverend Gayton, who walked with a cane, started drinking. Carolyn and I were upstairs in our bedroom playing when we saw him out the window. Suddenly he became animated, threw his cane away, and started cursing at the top of his voice and walking toward the house. That's when we locked our door and stayed at the window until we saw Daddy arrive home. "Daddy! Daddy!" We were screaming loud enough for the whole neighborhood to hear. When he drove up, we were overjoyed, knowing our protector had arrived.

Because of his recordings, Daddy was the most nationally celebrated minister in Detroit. But there were other highly respected clergymen whose churches were as well attended as ours: Reverend James Lofton, Reverend Chapman—whose theme song, "The Traveling Shoes Man," was also his nickname—and the flamboyant Prophet Jones, who enjoyed a huge following and will be remembered.

Prophet Jones lived in a large home on Arden Park and Woodward, only a block away from us. On my way to school I would walk past his house and marvel at how, every few months, he changed the color of the exterior. His house was as colorful as his personality. Prophet Jones was also famous for a long red carpet that was spread before him as he walked to his pulpit. He brought the carpet along wherever he preached, and no one could walk on that carpet except him. When he spoke at our church, though, he broke the rules for Daddy—Daddy was allowed to walk on the red carpet—a sign of Prophet Jones's respect.

Reverend Chapman and his wife were prominent in the African American community and, from time to time, would take me and Carolyn out for ice cream or lunch at Belle Isle, a pastoral island park in the middle of the Detroit River out on the East Side where the brothers and sisters gather annually. There was also another Reverend Franklin—M. L. Franklin—who lived on the West Side and was friends with Daddy. Sometimes people confused the two Franklins. We occasionally worshipped with Reverend M.L., who had two daughters, Louise and Cynthia, and a son, Larry.

For several years Beatrice Buck was my father's personal secretary. I remember Bea not only for her service and friendship with Daddy but for her shoe obsession as well. Little Sammy Bryant, one of the great singers from New Bethel, used to tell her famous story about Bea going with Daddy to Miami, where she bought ten pairs of shoes and wore every one before the day was over. Bea was the queen of shoes. These days she's a member of the Balentine Belles, a group associated with the former queen of the blues, Dinah Washington. Bea is a Detroit historian, and I often enjoy her reminiscing about my hometown's fascinating past.

Every now and then Daddy took time off to travel. He and Clara Ward once made an extensive tour of the Middle East. There was great excitement surrounding that trip. Daddy had long dreamed of visiting the Holy Land and walking in the footsteps of Jesus. I remember the beautiful postcards they sent from Egypt and Israel.

Later I saw photos of them on camels in the desert. When he and Clara returned, they were radiantly happy, carrying all sorts of presents for us, including gold-sequined shoes with tightly woven wedged heels and jackets and silk scarves of silver and gold.

Some people have speculated about whether my father and Clara Ward were intimate. I have no knowledge of that. I know they appreciated each other and recognized their mutual gifts of the ministry and song. They shared great times and loads of laughter. I would not have minded had they married, but it was not meant to be.

# Landscape of
# My Childhood

~

Detroit was a city known for beautiful snowfalls. A lot of people detested the snow, but I loved watching it softly fall over the city; I loved the texture of snow and the fun of sloshing and slipping around in it. I also loved snow ice cream and learned the recipe early on. (A tip: Don't use yellow snow. Use the clean, freshly fallen snow, Pet milk, eggs, sugar, and vanilla extract. It's some of the best ice cream you'll ever eat, significantly different from hand churned.)

During summer Detroit could be charming. Occasionally Daddy would take us for a ride to Belle Isle. We oohed and aahed at the sprays of water as it changed colors in the beautiful fountain that greeted us just as we crossed the bridge. It was quite a scene: the dancing water under a flood of moonlight, gorgeous weather, other families scattered along the waterside, BBQ ribs and loud voices on the wind, the kids with their radios blasting some funky R&B or the cool cats listening to jazz on WJZZ, and people chillin' or partying throughout the park.

The Gotham Hotel was another magical spot in the city of my

childhood. Whether on a frosty night in winter or a balmy evening in summer, the Gotham sparkled like a jewel. With its European styling and graceful decor, it was a symbol of elegance. John White, the African American owner, maintained his establishment impeccably. Sometimes we would sit in the car and wait for Daddy to visit his friends in the hotel; sometimes he would stand outside the hotel, bathed in a soft yellow light from overhead, as he laughed and conversed with friends and acquaintances. If it was summer, the top would be down on his Cadillac convertible, the hotel sparkling at sundown. Other times Daddy would walk us through the lobby and let us buy little candies at the gift shop.

You might see anybody at the Gotham—Marian Anderson, Sammy Davis, Dinah Washington, Roy Wilkins. The extravagant suites were named after jazz royalty—Duke Ellington and Count Basie. I was observant; I noticed the crisp white linen in the dining room and appreciated the formal look of it all, the warmth of families dining together.

You can imagine how excited I was when one day Daddy announced we were going to visit Miss Dorothy Donegan, who was staying at the Gotham. Miss Donegan was a virtuoso jazz pianist in the style of Art Tatum, and my father wanted her to hear me play. When we walked into Miss Donegan's suite, the first thing I noticed was a grand piano. She greeted us with a big smile before sitting down to play. She played so well—so beautifully and fluently—that when it was my turn, I played, but not nearly that well. At age ten, I couldn't begin to follow Dorothy Donegan.

Detroit in the fifties was still a safe place for children. We felt free to walk wherever we wanted. Catching the bus and the streetcar for ten cents a ride was an adventure. Every summer I'd ride the trolley all the way to Woodward and 8 Mile for the State Fair. I was enchanted by the sights and sounds and irresistible snacks—the French fries with white vinegar, the cotton candy, the little necklaces with inscriptions to your sweetie, the midway with the games of chance. My enchantment would be so deep that I'd spend all my money, including carfare, and be forced to walk all the way home, a hike that took hours.

Parents weren't afraid to have their kids run errands for them. And I was so proud Daddy trusted me at such a young age to venture far from home to run his errands. Sometimes he'd put me in a cab with an order for the House of Sides on John R, where all they served were soul side dishes. Most of my errands, though, were in our neighborhood. Oakland was the main street—we lived just off Oakland—and Oakland was a world of its own.

The gypsies, with their coal black hair and dark, dark eyes, were a strong presence on Oakland. They enticed you in to take your picture, three or four for a quarter, or to have your palm read. And there was the older man we called Mr. I Got It. He would dance up and down Oakland for hours shouting, "I got it! I got it!" What we didn't know then was that he had the number; Mr. I Got It was a numbers runner long before the lotto.

I also got hot dogs for Daddy from the kosher butcher. They were the best because they popped and crunched when you bit into them. The kosher butcher was also where I'd watch them grab a fresh chicken by the neck, swing it around, pop the neck, and start skinning, feathers flying everywhere over a huge barrel full of smelly dead birds—*whew!* Sometimes Daddy would send me down to the Log Cabin for barbecue. And across the street was the Champion Bar, a loud and raucous hangout. I never went in, of course, but sometimes I saw people being thrown out the front door, like in the old western movies.

I'll never forget Mr. Barthwell's drugstore. Mr. Barthwell was among the first black businessmen in Detroit to own a chain of stores. His ice cream was heavenly. Many were the times I went to Heckleman's grocery, where my dad had an account, to buy those products so typical of the fifties—Argo starch, Ivory Snow, Lux Flakes, and Bon Ami cleanser.

Big Mama did not hesitate to send me out for her dipping snuff. This was some wretched stuff, but Big Mama had to have it. I also frequented Mrs. Wiggins's sweetshop and whirled around on the new swivel seats while waiting for a milk shake or a sundae. Mrs. Wiggins's was on the corner of Oakland and Belmont, and Smokey Robinson stayed only a few doors down Belmont.

Smokey is my forever friend. We grew up together. Everyone loved Smokey. He became my brother Cecil's closest buddy and, as everyone knows, a major and most loved musical star. Smokey was full of fun and another one of the people to come out of our North End neighborhood and make it big. Others, just to name a few, were Diana Ross, the Four Tops, and Jackie Wilson. There was no place like the North End.

The North End was Red's Shine Parlor. While we listened to Lionel Hampton vibing on "Stardust," I sat on the shoestand watching Lester work out. Lester was Red's fine-looking assistant—*ooooooeeeeee!*—and I appreciated *all* his attributes. Everyone, including the future mayor Coleman Young, sent their shoes to Red's to get shined up, and they still do today. The Echo movie theater was only eight blocks down Oakland from our home; admission was a dime. That's where I first heard the song "La Vie en Rose," in a French movie. I've never forgotten it. Many years later, when I sang the song in Paris, I thought of the Echo Theater, where I sat in the dark as a tiny child and absorbed that memorable and haunting melody.

Oakland was one scene; Hastings was another. Hastings was where Daddy had built his church. Hastings was rougher and a little more exotic than Oakland. Hastings was the heart of Detroit's hottest entertainment strip; Hastings was also known for what was called the sporting life. Hastings was the area of the Flame Show Bar—actually on John R and Canfield a few blocks away—where big-name stars of rhythm and blues and jazz would strut their stuff. "Hastings," said Daddy, "is a fine place for a church because the church is for everyone."

Church was never more beautiful than during candlelight services. In darkness the choir entered from the rear, each member holding a flickering candle while singing "Jesus Is the Light of the World." I can still see the church awash in shadows and music. Many years later I echoed that refrain in my second gospel album, *One Lord, One Faith, One Baptism,* which I produced.

I remember Daddy in the pulpit, offering a history lesson. His text was from Deuteronomy: "The eagle stirreth her nest." "The eagle," he said, "is used as a symbol of God. In picturing God as an eagle stirring her nest, I believe history has been one big nest that God has been eternally stirring to make man better—and to help us achieve world brotherhood. The eagle is swift . . . the eagle is strong . . . the eagle has extraordinary sight. . . .

"My soul
 is an eagle
 in the cage that the Lord
 has made for me
 My soul
 my soul

is caged in this old body
And one of these days
the man who made the cage
will open the door
and let my soul
go
Yes He will
You ought to be able
to see me
take the wings of my soul
Yes, yes,
Yes!
Yes, one of these days
one of these old days
one of these old days
did you hear me say it?
I'll fly away and be at rest
When troubles and trials are over
when toils and tears are ended
when burdens are through burdening
my soul will take wings
Oh!
Oh, a few more days
a few more days!"

And the congregation said, "Yes," and my dad said, "Yes," and the candles were still burning, flames of love strong in the house of the Lord.

"The Eagle Stirreth Her Nest" went on to be my father's most famous sermon, a sacred text now included in anthologies of

African American literature taught in many colleges around the world.

After church many of the key members went to Stanley's, a hot Oriental restaurant a few blocks away. Stanley's served the best Chinese food in the city. Daddy, on the other hand, might drive farther down Hastings to Joe's record shop, known as JVB. Joe Von Battle was the first person to record my father's evening sermons. Daddy liked listening to the sermon he had delivered earlier that day. Joe had outdoor speakers, and sometimes when he played these sermons crowds formed on the street just to listen.

As I said before, church music wasn't the only style I absorbed as a child. There was the time, for instance, I was at the house of Erma's friend Wiladene Freeman when I heard a sound coming out of her record player. Never heard anything like it before. It was the most soulful voice I'd ever heard from any man with the exception of my father. This man was crying, "Come back, baby."

"Who is that?" I asked Wiladene.

"Girl," she said, "you mean you've never heard of Ray Charles?"

"No," I said softly, but I sure was enjoying him.

Ray became a favorite in the Franklin household. I remember one night when all of us, including Big Mama, had gone to bed. The house was pitch-dark, but we had left the hallway radio on. All the doors to the bedrooms were open. Out of the dark came Ray singing "Drown in My Own Tears." At the end Ray falls into a call-and-response with the crowd, getting them to say, "Yeah!" Well, the "Yeahs" went on for so long, until out of the darkness came the command of Big Mama, shouting at the top of her voice, *"Turn it off!"*

The new rhythm and blues, though, couldn't be turned off. "Frantic" Ernie Durham was the hottest jock in town. He played all of the newest records—"Why Don't You Write Me?" by the Jacks, "Why Oh Why" by the Kings, "A Kiss from Your Lips" by the Flamingos. By now you can appreciate my romantic involvement with these songs. One of the first secular songs to captivate me was "Stop, Pretty Baby, Stop." Wow, what a record! I was equally captivated by certain R&B piano pieces, like Lloyd Glenn's "Chica Boo." That song stayed with me forever.

Daddy never limited my musical loves; he appreciated some of the same music. He embraced the full range of African American culture. His record collection included Billy Eckstine, Nat "King" Cole, Mahalia and Clara and Arthur Prysock. Prysock, a wonderful jazz singer and devout Christian, sang at New Bethel whenever he was in town.

There was music coming from the street, music coming out the jukeboxes, music coming out of those old antique radios and first portable radios. "Have Mercy, Baby" by the Dominoes. Ruth Brown talking about "(Mama) He Treats Your Daughter Mean." Little Willie John singing "Talk to Me, Talk to Me." Harvey and the Moonglows reciting the "Ten Commandments of Love."

Meanwhile, the musical commandments of church were making equally strong impressions on me. There were no ifs, ands, or buts about it: *We had to be in church every Sunday morning and every Sunday evening.* I got deeper into church, both the music and the message. At age ten I was baptized at New Bethel. Big Mama cried as I accepted Jesus Christ as my Lord and personal Savior. I knew she was proud of me, but I didn't understand why she cried. Now, of course, as an adult and a mother, I do. I was proud of myself. Earlier I was given a small white Bible for knowing my lessons the best in Bible class.

My informal studies as a gospel singer benefited from the arrival of a young man from Chicago named James Cleveland. James helped shape my basic musical personality in profound ways. James was a gospel genius. He was one of those people modernizing gospel while honoring its traditional soul and message. As choir director, writer, arranger, pianist, singer, and, ultimately, minister, James became a giant of the black church. Before it was over, he'd be crowned King of Gospel. I was blessed to meet James so early in his career; he was barely out of his teens when he came to live with us in Detroit and accept his position as minister of music for New Bethel.

Daddy recognized James's talent. He had played piano for the Caravans and also for Mahalia Jackson. By the time he was only sixteen, James had written "Grace Is Sufficient," recorded by the great Roberta Martin Singers. He wrote hundreds of songs, many of which—"Walk On by Faith," "He's Using Me," and the magnificent "Peace, Be Still"—became gospel standards. His piano technique was pure gospel, with big chords that were exciting and rich. James heard harmonies in his head that most people missed. Plus, as a natural leader, he was the catalyst for dozens of vocal groups and choirs, including ours.

Of all his groups, though, none was better than the one composed of just James and his sister. They were sensational, and one of the very first gospel groups I'd ever heard. After I heard them there was no question that music was made for me.

James didn't have a naturally glorious voice. It was husky and hoarse, but, believe me, he could work it. With his supersoulful delivery, James could wreck a church in a matter of minutes. James and his friend Melvin Rencher, another great gospel artist and pianist, got together and helped to build up the New Bethel music program. Those were days when our home kicked into musical overdrive. Music poured from every room. Erma was practicing, James was rehearsing, Cecil might be listening to jazz upstairs . . . all was right with the world. . . .

Until the day Daddy left for church and noticed a couple of banana puddings his friend Lola was whipping up for us. He looked forward to eating the puddings that night. But when he arrived back home for dinner, they were gone. I'm sure he was working on radar to locate the desserts. After searching through the kitchen, he moved on to the rest of the house. Finally, he knocked on the door of James and Melvin's room and discovered two empty pudding dishes under James's bed. That was the end of James and Melvin living with us. The musical geniuses had to find lodgings elsewhere.

Daddy loved his banana pudding, and he also loved the prizefights. He loved the old Gillette fights. The big news of 1953 might have centered on the coronation of Queen Elizabeth II of England, but in our living room in Detroit, we were concentrating on the kings of the ring. Some of the warmest memories of my childhood center around our Emerson radio and, later, Wednesday night Gillette fights on TV. Fight night was and is a big night in the Franklin home. There'd be popcorn and hot dogs and screaming and cheering. I remember Joe Louis, Sugar Ray Robinson, Johnny Braton, Rocky Graziano, Rocky Marciano, and Kid Gallivan and his infamous Bolo Punch, Archie Moore the Mongoose. Inspired by my dad's love of the sport, I've been a lifelong fight fan myself. Today my favorites are Muhammad Ali, Tommy Hearns, Marvin Hagler, Big George Foreman, Larry Holmes, and Evander Holyfield. The greatest fight ever and greatest first and second rounds in history were between Hearns and Hagler. But in terms of all-time champs, Joe Louis was the most awesome; I've never seen a fighter back up and whip a man like Joe did. Ordinarily a man would be coming at you to punish you in that way.

In contrast to fight night, our Boston Boulevard home was also the scene of many Sunday afternoon church ladies' tea parties. I was part of the cleanup crew and didn't mind because I got to munch the best of the tea sandwiches, beautifully created with colored breads of pink and green by Sylvia Penn and Mrs. Eliza Butler and other ladies from the church.

In contrast to church tea parties, Daddy would sometimes have company from out of town, like Mahalia Jackson or Oscar Peterson. I was interested in taking a peek at the guests. I'd sit on top of the staircase and look through the banister at the activity below. There was always music, chatter, and warm laughter. Once I recall seeing the Queen of the Blues herself, Miss Dinah Washington, right below me. And what a surprise to watch, from my unseen vantage point, as she was being carried out of the house by Ted White, a man I would one day marry. To this day I don't know why White was carrying her out, though I suspect Dinah may have gotten overzealous.

Most days, of course, weren't that exciting. I had my little routine. I often had my lunch sitting in front of the TV watching Soupy Sales, a local favorite. I also never missed *Kukla, Fran & Ollie.* I was part of the first generation of kids addicted to the small screen. Game shows like *Beat the Clock* and melodramas like *I Remember Mama.* Later on I'd become a lifelong soapie, loving the endless twists and turns of *Search for Tomorrow*—with Stu, Ellen, and David and Joanne Tate—*The Young and the Restless,* and *The Bold and the Beautiful.*

❧

The facts of young womanhood came as a surprise to me. I was playing one afternoon when I was introduced to a monthly visitor. Because my mom wasn't there to explain what was happening, I thought I was dying. Fortunately, I got some quick education and realized that I would live. I was growing up.

I was certainly regarding the opposite sex with more interest. My first infatuation was with Samuel "Billy" Kyles, later Reverend Billy Kyles of Operation PUSH, the Memphis branch. My father often opened his pulpit to aspiring young ministers, and Billy arrived in Detroit with the Thompson Community Choir of Chicago. I was inspired by his rousing version of "Never Grow Old." I loved Billy's voice. I might have been nine or ten, while he was approximately nineteen. But when I saw he had brought his fiancée along, my unspoken reaction was *What did he bring her for?* She, however, was really a lovely person. Consequently, I sacrificed the great teenybop love of my life to a better and older woman. Billy and I are still friends today, and I have the greatest admiration for him. He was there at one of the most important times in my life: When my dad was gravely ill, he came to California and prayed with me before his surgery. I will always appreciate the great comfort his company gave me. Billy is one of the few real men I have ever known.

Big changes were just ahead of me. The teen years. Other than church and school and light housework, the main arena of my teen life was the local roller-skating rink.

Welcome to the Arcadia.

# "Let's Go Around Together"

~

Round and round and round, the rhythm of the Arcadia was the rhythm of LaVern Baker's "Jim Dandy," Dinah Washington's "Let's Go Around Together," Frankie Lymon and the Teenagers' "Why Do Fools Fall in Love?" and Johnny Ace's "Pledging My Love." My ice-skating model was Sonja Henie. I tried to emulate her and wound up with legs in the air; I looked like a newborn colt trying to stand.

During the summer, even though Carolyn, Cecil, Smokey, Bubbles (Wilbourne Kelly, my buddy and main man), Chuck Mixon, and Edward Brown pitched horseshoes in the old rabbit field next door to our home, it was roller skating that demanded my attention. Hula hoops may have been the rage all over the country, but Detroit was skating territory. Detroiters were serious skaters. My girlfriend and I planned our weekends and some weekdays around the Arcadia, chattering about what we were going to wear and how we were going to wear it—pedal pushers or a very tight skirt with four or five pairs of socks rolled down around the ankles. White bucks or checker boots, which I loved more than anything else, with chains hanging from the sides.

When Big Mama braided my hair, I wouldn't argue, but as soon as I got far enough away from the house, I unbraided it, let it down, and put on a little lipstick.

I'd take the trolley. The Arcadia was on Woodward, the main drag, the Champs-Élysées of Detroit. When I'd hit the door, I'd hear Dinah or the Drifters blasting over the loudspeakers, and I couldn't wait to get in and lace up my skates, stopping in the skate room up front to see what was new.

The Arcadia was young love in bloom. And the young brothers of the day were . . . _oh, my God!_ If anyone warned me to proceed with caution, the warning fell on deaf ears. The finest brothers in the city were all there, cruising the rink from one end to the other.

The floor was the size of a small football field, with a curtained stage and an organ at the far end. I skated on Tuesdays, Wednesdays, Fridays, Saturdays, and sometimes Sundays. We were so innocent, young black America at its best—tight knits, ponytails, Tycora (a nylon-feeling fabric) sweaters, hoop skirts, saddle oxfords. Randel and Kirk Pierson, James and Barbara Crumby, Claudette Crumby, Mary Alice, Jackie Martin, Tommy Lee, and Edward and Floyd Jordan were some of the regulars and my closest friends. It was a sepia scene of budding adolescence, all-American teenage stuff, sipping on cherry Cokes or hugged up as we skated during couples-only, listening to Dinah asking the musical question, "Did you say I got a lot to learn?" Well, honey, teach me tonight. Treasured memories: walking down Woodward at midnight in the warm summer air with our skate wheels tucked in our back pockets headed toward Tops for hamburgers and laughing and kidding and sometimes stealing a kiss or two. Those were the days . . . the thrills!

Sometimes we'd stop by White Castle instead of Tops and get a bag of spiced ham sandwiches and wash 'em down with Vernors ginger ale, the best ginger ale in the country and a Detroit exclusive even now.

Jackie Martin and Jerry Bailey were my best friends. We'd go home after skating all evening and call each other and talk about the highlights of the day. Sitting on my dad's front porch as suspicious-looking cars drove by with fellows hanging out the windows, Jerry and I would daydream about the future. We were definitely interested in the opposite sex, and I remember Janie Martin, Jackie's sister, in hot pursuit of a fellow named Bert until she finally caught and married him.

The fellas were going through growing pangs of their own, and some of them, like Kirk Pierson, tried to be more adult and sophisticated. Kirk was always asking us if we wanted to have a cup of coffee after walking him home. Coffee? We didn't drink coffee; we wanted Cokes and milk shakes. Coffee was for old folks.

My heartthrob was one of the smoothest sweet-talking players of the day. While he was seeing me, he was involved with at least three other girls at the same time. I suspected it at the time, but my suspicions melted away when he flashed that smile.

Lester had to be the finest brother alive on the North End; Lester did all kinds of good things for Red's Shine Parlor. However, one evening Lester came over, confronting me with something a girl claimed I had said. Suddenly he shoved me, and just as he did Cecil was coming out of the house. Within seconds he and Cecil went to war.

But it didn't end there. After that a group of us, some fifteen strong, took it up Oakland. We were looking for the girl who had told the lie on me. Finally we ran into her, and she denied it. Then the argument began. As we started back down Oakland, I turned and swung at her. I missed—*oh, shit*—and the fight was on. We rolled out into the middle of Oakland, stopping traffic in both directions. I mean, we were throwing down toe to toe. I was making full use of some of those Sugar Ray Robinson techniques I had come to know. That evening we lit up the neighborhood.

Cecil always looked out for me. He scrutinized my boyfriends. If he didn't think they were cool, he'd let me know—or try to pull my coat in different ways. Rather than make blatant statements, he said enough to make me think twice. After that he never interfered; Cecil trusted my judgment.

Cecil was also enterprising. He and Pete Moore, who later formed the Miracles with Smokey, ran a thriving business in our first-floor bathroom. They processed guys' hair. The bathroom was tiny, not even enough room for two chairs, but they did a brisk business, shaping beautiful finger waves. They turned into expert amateurs, and all the brothers in the neighborhood came by on the weekends to get ready. Word went out that Cecil and Pete could work.

Cecil also admired some of the true masters of the process, like Benny Mullins and Ples Joy over on Twelfth Street and Sylvester Moore on Linwood. As a process man, Benny was as bad as he wanted to be—and still is.

Of course I loved the neighborhood beauty shop, where ladies would come in and out with big brown bags full of merchandise while we sat under the dryers, oohing and aahing over the fabulous clothes. The dish was deep in the beauty shop. Pinky Boldin, the hot beautician of the day, brought in the contemporary windblown look for young black women. She was the queen of modern hair; her thing was Lustrasilk. Pinky also loved the bluesman T-Bone Walker, and whenever T was due in Detroit, she would be bright-eyed and buzzing. "T-Bone's coming to town, T-Bone's coming to town," she'd declare. Detroit had a long love affair with the electric bluesmen of the fifties, giants like T-Bone, B. B. King, and Bobby "Blue" Bland, who was influenced by my father. (I recently read an interview with Blue where he specifies copying Daddy's squall from "The Eagle Stirreth Her Nest.")

I fell in love with the Lustrasilk look, the perm applied by Pinky. Lustrasilk turned your hair supersilky. It also turned Daddy red when he saw the bills—a Lustrasilk was expensive—so he quickly phoned Pinky, instructing her to lighten up and find more modest ways of making us look pretty.

I appreciated glamour. I read *Modern Screen* and *Silver Screen* magazines. These were the movie publications that followed the careers and lives of golden-era movie stars like Lana Turner, Bette Davis, and Barbara Stanwyck. Of the young stars, I liked Elizabeth Taylor and, in my age-group, Sandra Dee. Sandra's *A Summer Place* with Troy Donahue remains one of my favorite movies. Jean Louis created Sandra's wardrobe, clothes to die for. Later in my career, when I performed for the Queen Mother of England and Prince Charles, I wore a Jean Louis gown of white chiffon and nude souf-flé. A dream come true.

The biggest heartthrob of my teen years, though, wasn't to be found in the roller rink or the halls of Hutchins Junior High. He was to be found in church. He was a singer and a star, one of the finest brothers ever to grace New Bethel. When I first saw him, all I could do was sigh; my unspoken response as I looked back over my shoulder was, *Oh my God—who is that?*

When I saw him and his brother L.C. coming down the aisle for that evening's program, I got happy long before the singing started.

I'm talking about Sam Cooke.

# The Soul Stirrer

It must have been around 1955 or '56. Daddy was backing the presidential candidacy of Governor Adlai Stevenson. Daddy was a staunch, lifelong Democrat, as am I. But back then, when I was a girl growing up on the North End of Detroit, politics were way over my head, while music hit me right at home.

I loved the secular music played by Rocking with Leroy—Little Willie John, the Flamingos, the Moonglows, and the Spaniels. But it was at Daddy's church that another sound and sight really rocked my world. It was during one of the gospel programs at New Bethel that I was introduced to the Soul Stirrers. One Stirrer stirred me more than the rest.

Some men can sing, charm, and shine; some are easy with their good looks, others radiate confidence. Sam had all of this and more—the personality of a prince and a voice to match. He was one in a million. Yet for all his abundant talent, he exuded simple humility, the sign of a great person. He treated everyone with respect. His manners were impeccable. Sam was in a class by himself.

I had heard the Soul Stirrers, on record and the radio, before that evening I saw them in church. Male quartets were a major part of the golden age of gospel. The great groups like the Swan Silvertones produced great lead singers like Claude Jeter, who, along with Ira Tucker of the Dixie Hummingbirds and Julius Cheeks of the Sensational Nightingales, were monuments of pure gospel power. Beyond the enormity of their voices and the mastery of their technique, the groups they led had a new and spirited style. Rather than robes, the men might wear matching green or blue or even gold suits. They had their own kind of choreographed steps. They were servants of God, to be sure, but they were also showmen.

Among the great groups of gospel, the women, by contrast, wore lavishly colorful robes and sometimes dress suits, like Ruth "Baby Sister" Davis of the Davis Sisters—Jackie, Audrey, Alfreda, and Curtis Dublin—a very powerful and spirit-filled group, and Dot Love and the Gospel Harmonettes, whom I particularly liked. I also considered Jackie Verdell of the Davis Sisters one of the best and most underrated female soul singers of all time. It was through Jackie that I learned the expression "Girl, you peed tonight"— meaning you were dynamite. Several nights Jackie sang so hard she literally had a spot or two on her robe from peeing. Singing far too hard, I also peed here and there in the early days; I quickly realized no one should sing that hard.

Sam Cooke never sang too hard. He sang hard occasionally, though, and when he did you were in for the best time of your life. Later, of course, Sam would become a major crossover star in the world of pop. But to hear him during his gospel days was a special thrill. His biggest hits were "Nearer to Thee," "Wonderful," and

"Touch the Hem of His Garment." As I mentioned, I established myself by singing my first solo in church, "Jesus Be a Fence Around Me," because I loved the Soul Stirrers' version so much.

Sam was love on first hearing, love at first sight. That Sunday evening he and L.C. were outfitted in dark-brown-and-blue supersharp trench coats that had a foreign intrigue about them.

Sam was certainly an inspiration to me. I was so influenced by him that Daddy told me to stop emulating Sam and instead express my own heart and soul. I'm so thankful today for my father's advice.

I'd have to say that James Cleveland, because he was so much a part of our lives, was a more direct influence on me than Sam. James was also a righteous teacher and organized a nameless trio consisting of me, Laura Lee Rundless, and Jackie Burney. We styled ourselves after the Caravans' numbers like "Lord, Keep Me Day by Day" or "Running for Jesus," records I played so much the black grooves turned white. James had a keen instinct for vocal arrangements; he'd give us our notes and create a beautiful blend. Later, he'd also help the Meditation Singers, a soulful gospel group featuring a young Della Reese and Earnestine Rundless, Laura Lee's godmother. Eventually Laura Lee became a Meditation Singer herself.

While I was surrounded by gospel group sounds, I also enjoyed the boy and girl doo-wop groups I heard over the loudspeaker at the Arcadia. They very accurately expressed some of my youthful emotions. I could directly relate to these songs of love and palpitations of the heart. I loved the Falcons' "He's So Fine" and was impressed by their lead singer, Wilson Pickett, one of the great soul singers. I also liked Frankie Lymon and Little Willie John, brother of Mable John and master soul singer. Hopefully, the R&B Pioneer

Awards and the Rock and Roll Hall of Fame awards will remember Little Willie John's "Talk to Me, Talk to Me" and "All Around the World" and so many other hits he recorded. Finally, Ruth Brown's fabulous "5-10-15 Hours."

The boys were hanging out on street corners, back porches, and basements—and so were the girls. Erma formed a group with me, Wiladene Freeman, and Jackie Burney. We worked up a female rendition of Lloyd Price's "Lawdy Miss Clawdy." And we knew we were good. We weren't serious enough to sing anywhere outside of the house, but the experience of honing harmonies was an essential part of my musical education.

Music everywhere. The street-corner doo-wop. Sarah Vaughan's bebop flowing from Cecil's attic apartment. The choirs, the organs, the brothers and sisters spreading the gospel from various churches. My sister Erma, an engaging and excellent singer herself, was the first in our family to head into the secular field. My sister Carolyn, an excellent singer too, would also make pop records for RCA Records.

Early on a young man named Berry Gordy, Jr., and his partner, Billy Davis, came by the house and played their songs on the little upright piano in our back room. Erma made some demos for them. Berry had written some tunes for Jackie Wilson, like "Lonely Teardrops" and "To Be Loved," which were getting airplay. This was years before Motown. I saw Berry as a good-looking, nice, and aggressive young man. I also had met his sisters Anna and Gwen and knew them as stylish women who ran a photo concession at the Flame Show Bar.

The Gordy sisters were very savvy and straight-ahead. I recall opening the door for Anna when she came to visit my dad. She and Daddy had a special friendship, and I always appraised her coif, makeup, and fashionable dress. She had a beautiful black leather coat with an alpaca sailor collar and tie that I would have bought off of her at a moment's notice. I never saw Esther Gordy as much as I did Gwen and Anna, but in later years I would come to know her a little better.

Long before I performed at the Flame, I'd ride by on the way to church. The doors would be wide open, and I'd hear the rehearsals or performances inside and breathe in the smell of the evening before. I also loved the food at the hot tamale stand on the corner that served up the best little greasy bags of steamed shrimp flavored with cayenne pepper.

Berry Gordy had a feel for modern melodies, and he looked to Erma as one of his prime interpreters. Erma was a very good interpreter of lyrics. In fact, she recorded the initial version of Berry's "All I Could Do Was Cry." Unfortunately, Erma's version didn't make it on the radio before Etta James's. Etta had the hit.

All the Franklin sisters had spunk, Erma no less than the rest. Even after Motown started up, Erma never signed, not because Berry didn't want her but because she wanted to see the world in her own way.

Mainly, though, our world was forged by our father. His influence prevailed. For example, Daddy firmly believed in education; he also believed in the benefits black students derive from black colleges. He felt Cecil and Erma would be more inclined to study in a Southern environment, and he was right. That isn't to say I couldn't or wouldn't excel in the college atmosphere—I was an excellent student and double-promoted several times—but later it was my final decision not to reenroll in high school. Daddy felt my gift should be nurtured and developed in churches and auditoriums, wherever gospel was performed.

Carolyn thought she knew what was best for her. She wanted to take tap dancing. But Daddy wanted her to take piano. For a while Carolyn's friend Bennie was teaching both of us tap steps. We were loving it. Once Daddy found out, though, it was all over. He took Carolyn's tap shoes and threw them out the back door. "There will be no tap dancers in here," he said. And there weren't.

One evening Erma and I went to the Warfield Theater to see the talent show we had heard so much about. Little Willie John was starring that night, singing "Fever" as only he could, "Talk to Me, Talk to Me," and "All Around the World" (with those unforgettable lyrics, "Grits ain't groceries, eggs ain't poultry and Mona Lisa was a man"). Without a doubt he was one of the most soul-satisfying singers of our generation. There were also shake dancers and the funnyman Winehead Willie (Bill Murray), who in a few years would emcee many of the Motown shows. Erma and I had a ball, and we were in no hurry to leave. We weren't even thinking about going home till we checked the time and panicked.

When we arrived, Daddy wouldn't let us in. We frantically rang the bell and banged on the door. He opened the window and asked us what time it was before telling us, "If you're going to be coming in this late, go back where you came from." With that, his French window closed tight and the lights went out. We threw rocks and pebbles against Cecil's window, but Cecil wasn't about to go against Daddy. "I can't do that," he said. "You all sleep in the car." So that's what we did, for at least two hours, until Daddy relented and let us in. Lesson learned. Needless to say, we never did that again.

Other lessons didn't come as easily. When it came to romance, and to boys, my head was still in the clouds. Visions of superfine faces and physiques danced in my head. I hadn't been educated to the things that were really important where young men were concerned, or how to pick a good man, beyond what my dad used to call face and butt.

# Romeo of the
# Roller Rink

◦━◦

Was I innocent? Naïve? Vulnerable? Lovestruck?

Yes, all of the above.

I was a red-blooded African American teenage girl, in love with love and the dance of love. And a couple of those boys were really moving me. But let me make this clear—I was not boy crazy, and I was definitely a one-man young woman. You had to be extremely special to get my attention and meet my standards after some serious interaction and encounters.

This was the era when ballrooms were still in full flower. You could go to the Greystone (which Berry Gordy would eventually buy) or the Madison to hear Hank Ballard and the Midnighters or the Royal Jokers or the Penguins singing their heavenly "Earth Angel." The ballrooms were cool for the bop, slow dancing, and the infamous ballroom dance, but, as I've said, the Arcadia was the place for younger people to meet. Come rain or shine, heat wave or ice storm, we went to the Arcadia.

I was twelve when I first fell in love. My first serious boyfriend, whom I'll call Romeo, had a romantic aura about him. This was not a fly-by-night affair. He worked as an apprentice at a barbershop on Hastings near Hancock, where he also shined shoes and studied under a head first-chair barber. He was taller than I was and good-looking, with a head covered with beautiful waves. He had an easy way of conversing. During couples-only time at the Arcadia, we skated to songs like "Teach Me Tonight" and "The Cool Jerk." My hair was wretched at the end of the night, totally sweated out and pressed to the sides of my face from being hugged up.

Oh, those pink-and-blue-light parties in the basement! There'd be chicken frying and slow dancing, everyone ballrooming. The brothers would have you in a serious back bend doing the ballroom. No one in this country could ballroom like the men in Detroit.

We hung out at Tops and held hands walking down Woodward. Romeo called me almost every night and whispered sweet nothings in my ear. Sometimes we even hung on in silence for minutes at a time, in tune to the rhythm of each other's breathing. We were in love. And after a number of evenings together, that particular time of month didn't come as usual. I started humming and sweating the outcome.

Daddy had been telling me not to associate with the girl down the street, who he felt was too fast for me. Subsequently he noticed my weight gain and told me he was taking me to the doctor. Just as I suspected . . . I was pregnant.

Some other fathers have been known to put their daughters out of their homes, but not my dad. He was not judgmental, narrow, or scolding. He simply talked about the responsibilities of motherhood. He was a realist, and he expected me to face the reality of having a child. The days of spiced ham and Popsicles were over. I was becoming a young adult and a parent all at once.

For a short while, my boyfriend and I would meet in our backyard late at night and discuss the future. For a Detroit minute, we talked about running off to get married. Thank God we didn't, because Daddy would have killed him. My father knew we were far too young to make that kind of commitment. We hardly knew what commitment meant. In my fifth or sixth month, I dropped out of school. My family supported me in every way. The doctor put me on a special diet because I was gaining too much weight, but the pregnancy went very well. When my baby was born, I had just turned fourteen, not the easiest or best age to begin a family but a blessing nonetheless. All children are gifts from God; all children are miracles.

I accepted the blessing and named my son Clarence, after my dad. Everyone adored Clarence. He was a beautiful little baby with a beautiful temperament. I took him from one side of town to another so friends could see and hold him. I remember traveling over to the West Side to visit Carolyn, Vera, and Leslie Strong, sisters of Barrett Strong, one of my former classmates who wrote and sang "Money," an early Motown hit. Clarence was darling, and I cherished those quiet moments when he would sleep on my chest while I listened to the DeJohn Sisters singing "Lullabye of Love."

Big Mama and Erma were tremendously helpful. They pitched in. The romantic relationship that once burned so brightly burned out. But the love between a mother and a child is forever. This was my baby, I intended to love and care for him, and I did.

The contrast between a neglectful dad and a conscientious dad was something I couldn't ignore because of my own dad. His concern and participation in the lives of his children were exemplary. And even when his own career took off and he became a national figure in the African American church—and a recording star—he still performed the duties of a dad with patient love on the road and at home.

Daddy's spreading prominence began with the radio. He had had broadcasts in Memphis and Buffalo, and starting in 1952 the New Bethel services were broadcast over WJLB, Booth Broadcasting, in Detroit. Those broadcasts continued for decades, establishing his reputation in the local community.

Since 1953 Joe Von Battle had been recording Daddy's sermons. Through Chess Records of Chicago, Battles signed Daddy to a label contract. Chess was powerful in the African American community primarily for their blues artists—Muddy Waters, Howlin' Wolf, Sonny Boy Williamson—and, in the R&B field, Chuck Berry and Bo Diddley. They also recorded Harvey and the Moonglows and would later sign Etta James.

Daddy's albums, live recordings of his sermons at New Bethel, proved highly popular worldwide. And when WLAC-AM out of Gallatin, Tennessee, near Nashville, started playing them, they sold like wildfire throughout the country. Randy's Record Store sponsored the program, which, on a clear night, could be heard far and wide. Many a dark night as we drove down the highways of the Deep South we heard Randy's playing some of my favorite records, like Little Jimmy Brown and the Everly Brothers, as I gazed out into the dark night. Randy's also had a mail-order business and shipped Daddy's records, along with those of other artists, to every state. My father's fame spread. Over the years Chess would release more than sixty of his albums. It wasn't long before virtually every black church in America wanted Daddy to address their congregation. They wanted to see and hear the preacher now known as "the man with the million-dollar voice," who preached "The Eagle Stirreth Her Nest."

In his first travels my father worked with other gospel stars, not as the headliner but as an equal. He told the story, for instance, of how Mrs. Ward, Clara's business-savvy mother and manager of the world-famous Ward Singers, offered him five hundred dollars for an appearance at the city auditorium in Houston, his first out-of-state engagement. When he arrived at his hotel, he was told by another preacher that the Wards had never played so large a venue; previously they had performed at the high school. According to the preacher, it was Daddy's name that had sold out the auditorium.

Later that evening, all the maids in the hotel came to my daddy's room for his autograph. He was surprised that his reputation had preceded him. When he saw that six thousand people had paid between $2.50 and $3.50 a ticket, he approached Mrs. Ward and the promoter. "A fair fee for my appearance," he stated, "would be fifteen hundred dollars, not five hundred." They balked. Daddy calmly explained that his return ticket to Detroit was prepaid, and if fifteen hundred dollars was unacceptable, he would simply take an earlier plane. They met his price.

My father needed funds to supplement his New Bethel salary. In his autobiography, *Give Me This Mountain,* he wrote, "In a low-income congregation when they are paying you as a pastor, they resent the fact that you are calling upon them—in addition to what they are paying you—to help you educate your children. Because some of them have children for whom they are making no effort to educate, they resent you for asking them to help you educate your own. So the need for getting them through school motivated me to go out and try to make necessary monies to finance their education."

In the beginning, Daddy went out on the same program with the Dixie Hummingbirds and the Wards. After the groups sang, Daddy would close out with one of his stirring sermons. Soon, though, it became clear that he was the main attraction. It became more practical for him to put together his own package. That's what happened, and that's how I became part of my father's ministry. After my first child, he was concerned with overseeing my activities, and, because he felt I had the gift, he was also concerned with developing me as a singer.

His development as a minister never ceased to move and amaze me as I listened to his sermons in different auditoriums throughout the country. Sometimes I became concerned for people who were so passionately overcome with the Spirit that they seemed about to fall out of the balconies (but never did). The buildings always erupted with the joy of the Holy Ghost.

I cherish the memory of traveling with my father, stopping at little grocery stores in the Deep South and buying hog head cheese, commonly called souse, and saltine crackers with sandwich spread washed down with sodas . . . eating and laughing as we drove along.

I could travel because of Big Mama, who helped with Clarence. It was my debut as a professional. Daddy would pay me for every service. The churchgoing audiences in auditoriums all over the country were generous with their praise. They accepted me, encouraged me, and gave me the confidence to see me through the rest of my career. I'm grateful for the opportunity Daddy provided, and those special memories will always be treasured and alive in my heart.

# The Glory Road

The most I had ever traveled from Detroit was to Buffalo and Chicago. In fact, around this same time I went to Chicago, without Daddy, to sing in a program hosted by Mahalia Jackson. I was excited, and, even though Clara Ward was my number-one idol and mentor, I held Mahalia in high esteem. Mahalia was down-home and a devout Christian; she fondly told the story of wrestling alligators in her native New Orleans before she moved to Chicago. Mahalia had a depth of soul and a majesty about her. She was a pious woman and absolutely sincere; you felt how deeply she loved the Lord.

When she praised my performance and thanked me for coming, I took it as the highest compliment. After the concert, though, one small matter still lingered in my mind: I hadn't been paid. That evening I didn't say anything to Mahalia. I was just too shy to ask her for money. I looked up to her and found it hard to put my thoughts into words. This was my first time away from my dad, and I had no idea how to state my request. I was just hoping she'd hand me an envelope. I was all packed up and ready to head for the airport when I decided to call her. I really did want to get paid.

"Miss Jackson," I said.

"Yes, baby, what is it?"

"This is Aretha, and I just wanted to say that I'm leaving to go home."

"Well, that's fine, baby. Be sure and tell your daddy hello for me."

"I will."

"And . . . uh . . . Miss Jackson . . ."

"Yes?"

"I just wanted to say good-bye."

"Okay. Good-bye, Aretha, and thanks so much for coming."

Finally, I asked, "What do you want me to do, Miss Jackson?"

"What do I want you to do about what?" she asked. "Why, I want you to go home, baby. Everything is over."

"I mean about being paid."

"Okay, baby, I'll talk to your dad about it."

So I left Chicago with my heart broken.

When I left home with Daddy to appear on his gospel bill, we presented a full service in every city and at every venue. We were joined by two other singers, Sammy Bryant and Lucy Branch. Sammy was a midget in size only, about three and a half feet tall, and called the little lady with the big voice. Everyone loved Sammy. She had gusto and soul. You couldn't believe such a huge sound could come out of such a tiny frame, but, believe me, she could wreck a house and did just that with "I've Got a Home Somewhere in Heaven." Lucy Branch was a formidable vocalist herself.

I preceded my father's sermons. At this point I was accompanying myself on piano. By absorbing the James Cleveland style—big chords and dramatic flourishes—I was able to give myself strong keyboard support. I provided a solid foundation for my voice. Outside of church I also loved playing in other styles. By ear I learned the Erroll Garner jazz technique—Erroll was fabulous—with his raining tremolos and easy swing. I felt increasingly comfortable at the piano.

Inspired by Sammy, I did my best. By the time Daddy was ready to sermonize, the listeners were ready to receive the word. And while my dad spoke, I stayed at the piano, providing the right accents to underscore his message as I ad-libbed behind him. Like many preachers in the hallowed whooping style, he finished in a traditional chant. Sometimes after the sermon he would sing. As his accompanist, I was proud to assist him.

He could be talking about "The Man at the Pool," "Pressing On," "The Eagle Stirreth Her Nest," "The Prodigal Son," or "The Dry Bones in the Valley." Say it loud, I'm black and I'm proud. People used to show and express themselves so much more in those days than they do in churches today. Daddy brought many lost sheep back into the fold. He gave the worshippers everything he had—knowledge, wisdom, and the courage to go on. Certain sermons—"A Bigot Meets Jesus" is a beautiful example—became classic lessons in racial relations. Others, like "A Mother of the Cross," brought the meaning of Christ home to everyone.

We saw everyone on those tours, great gospel singers like the Davis Sisters of Philadelphia, who traveled with us often. I also saw the Jewel Gospel Singers at the Apollo in New York; these young girls could sing and shout. I especially liked Cassietta, whose voice was filled with feeling. Later Cassietta became known as Candi Staton in the secular arena, where she had a major hit—"Young

Hearts Run Free"—before returning to gospel. Many a night Cassietta and Saderia shook up the service singing "I Buckled Up My Shoes and I Started" or "Precious Lord."

I related to Cassietta as a Christian and a professional. And I say professional because when you are being paid to be somewhere on time, and carry yourself with pride and dignity, and to present yourself thoughtfully and responsibly, that's professional.

One rainy night on a dark Mississippi road, we pulled into a gas station in the middle of nowhere. So imagine how delighted we were when another car pulled in and we saw other black folks, the Stapleses—Mavis, Pervis, Yvonne, Cleotha, and Pops. What a beautiful coincidence! It's also what I would call destiny. The Staples were a very close-knit family who made stirring music. Their early records on Veejay were gospel evergreens. Pops's guitar, Mavis's lead vocals, and the uniqueness of the family harmony gave those songs a distinctive twang. The Stapleses' supertight harmonies were riveting. I especially loved "The Downward Road Is Crowded," "Unclouded Day," and "Will the Circle Be Unbroken."

Daddy had bought a silver 1957 El Dorado, one of the most beautiful cars I had ever seen. On occasion we were subjected to second-class treatment in the South in restaurants but always knew we were first-class people. We were also in the avant-garde of gospel performers, and proud of it.

I always enjoyed seeing the secular stars, singers I'd heard on records and the radio like Fats Domino, Bobby "Blue" Bland, whom I met in Jacksonville, and Carmen McRae, whom I saw in Newport News, Virginia. In our hotel in New Orleans, I saw the R&B diva Big Maybelle along with her little bitty boyfriend. Maybelle was one of the baddest singers ever. Her version of "Candy" is a classic; no one will ever sing "Candy" like Big Maybelle.

These were famous faces, sparkling personalities, all worlds away

from Detroit. And of course every time we ran into Sam Cooke, it was the ice cream on the cake. Sam was so cool I switched cigarette brands, giving up Kools for Kents because Sam smoked Kents. Whenever he was in the same city, we couldn't wait to see him. If the Soul Stirrers were on our program, my teenage heart was anything but still.

Once in Atlanta, where Herman Nash promoted us, we were all—the Staples, Sam, Daddy, and our group—at the Savoy Hotel. A little after midnight Sam passed my door on the way to his room. I was playing some of his records with my lights out when he heard them and knocked. We talked briefly as I stood in the doorway. The next day I walked down to his room to continue the conversation. We closed the door and were sitting on the bed; the room was quite small. We were talking innocuously when a thunderous knock came at the door. It was Daddy. Sam and I froze in our tracks. Daddy gave new meaning to waiting to exhale as he proclaimed, "Aretha, I know you're in there." Then I heard him ask the Stapleses if they had seen me. "No, Reverend," they said, "we haven't seen Aretha," even though they knew where I was. As soon as I heard Daddy's footsteps going back down the hallway, I shot out of Sam's room like a SCUD missile and ran back to mine, just when the conversation between me and Sam had taken another turn. Daddy never knew that with his intimidating knock he changed the course of history.

Not long after that Sam switched from gospel to pop. That switch had the gospel world buzzing. Daddy had told me the news, and, unlike some other ministers with a bias against pop, he was happy for Sam. The gospel singers couldn't talk about anything else. Audrey Davis of the Davis Sisters and I used to compare notes, and she was buzzing about how Sam had married his high school sweetheart and how gorgeous she was and how they were traveling with the baby and how he had bought them all a beautiful new home in California.

Whether he was married or not, Sam's music was still an important part of those early days for me. Erma had joined me and Daddy as a secretary of our gospel tour. One memory lingers: We were driving down some darkened highway somewhere in the South, rolling over skunks, whose odor hung in the air for miles. Suddenly out of the dark night we heard that voice; it was Sam singing "You Send Me." *Oh my God!* we screamed. *Oh no, oh no, it's his first pop record!* We were so excited we had to pull over. I mean, we were squealing and carrying on like typical teenage fans. You've seen the teenyboppers in the front rows and in the crowds with Sinatra, Elvis, and the Beatles—okay, that was Aretha and Erma listening to Sam. That night my sister and I realized we were the world's biggest Sam Cooke fans.

We were always talking about Sam. We followed the gossip, and when we learned he was going to be on national TV—*The Ed Sullivan Show* no less—we were giddy with anticipation. We were at the Savoy Hotel in Atlanta the night of his appearance. The only TV was in the lobby, and we were all crowded around the small set behind the front desk. All of us except Erma. Well, Erma finally showed up just a few minutes before the show, wearing a formal evening gown! I looked at her stunned. I couldn't stop laughing. What was she doing wearing an evening gown in this dinky little lobby? She was acting like we were at the Waldorf-Astoria. Unfortunately, Sullivan let Sam do only one song that night. As soon as we learned Sam wouldn't be returning for another number, the lobby erupted in protestations. We were screaming loud enough to be heard in New York.

Sometime later in the year, in the wake of the huge success of "You Send Me," Sam came to Detroit to play the Flame on John R.

Erma and I decided since he had gotten married we weren't going. We had turned in our Sam Cooke fan cards. How dare he have a wife!

He opened on a Friday night, and Erma and I sat out on the sunporch, halfway watching TV, declaring we were not going to the Flame, convincing ourselves that we had no further interest in a happily married Sam Cooke. That attitude, though, lasted no more than an hour. At some point Erma looked at me and I looked at her. The unspoken words coming out of our mouths were, *Who are we kidding? Let's go!* We dashed upstairs, dressed to the nines, arrived at the Flame, lied about our age, and caught Sam's last set, loving every second of it, cheering him on until we were hoarse. What a night! Sam could take you to the point where you would say to yourself, *If he keeps singing like that, somebody is gonna have to pick me up off the floor and call an ambulance because he's killing me!*

# Casanova Revisited

At age sixteen I was still attracted to the Arcadia. My friends and I were still wearing pink poodle skirts or skintight skirts with Tycora sweaters. And if you had no behind, you wore two skirts to make it look like more was going on. After buying the baby and myself a few things with the money I earned on the road with Daddy, I upgraded my skates and bought Raybestos, the Cadillac of wheels. Those wheels made me feel I was floating on a cloud; I was on a roll . . . so smooth.

I was also rolling toward a serious heartthrob of the roller rink, a fine young man who caught my eye and warmed my heart. He was a little older. He drove a sleek Ford Fairlane convertible and wore tight jeans and open-collared sweaters. He looked too good. Later his style changed to silk suits and Italian loafers. He worked that rink with such finesse that I didn't even realize he was working it. While the Flamingos cooed, "I only have eyes for you," I only had eyes for him.

We had long talks on the telephone nightly, so long that once I fell asleep on the phone. Sometimes we barely spoke; we just held the phone to our ears and grooved to each other's sensuous breathing, communicating by osmosis. The line was tied up so long and the bills were so high, Daddy finally took out the phone, forcing us to go to a pay phone or not call at all.

I had fallen in love with Casanova, beautiful waves and all. Soon we were sweethearts. By the time I discovered I was pregnant, though, I had also discovered that Casanova was less than true. He was playing me and just about every other female with two legs at the Arcadia. When I realized he was seeing several other young ladies, I knew my single-parent status would not be altered.

While I was pregnant, he would drive past the house with the top dropped, blow the horn, and keep going. I couldn't believe he was going to be this cold. He never stopped to spend any time or to check on my condition. Obviously, he wasn't that concerned. I was hurt and disillusioned. Yet, oddly enough, like many other women in similar circumstances, I still loved him for a while. Finally, though, I saw him for what he was—a big dog.

It wasn't easy telling my dad that, as a teenager, I was expecting my second child. But Daddy reinforced the attitude he had expressed earlier with his broad and sensitive understanding: As a family we stood together, supporting each other shoulder to shoulder. He never made a serious issue of it. His only lecture was that I be responsible and care for my children. Bravo, Daddy!

The pregnancy went well, and when my second son was born I named him Eddie, after his dad. However, there was no twilight sleep this time, a procedure that Daddy had secured for me the first time around to save me from the pain. Eddie was a natural birth. He was a sweet and beautiful infant with a gentle disposition, and another special joy in my life. According to Big Mama, Eddie was too small, so she set about fattening him up. I agreed with her and gave particular attention to his diet.

By now the Franklin family had moved from Boston Boulevard over to the West Side, to an estate home on LaSalle, an exclusive residential street with enormous lush trees and manicured lawns. LaSalle represented a major step up for my dad. It was the most beautiful home I had ever seen. His recordings and gifts as an orator and charismatic man of the cloth had resulted in a much-improved financial status for our family. He was able to buy a showplace designed along traditional lines and built in the early years of the century by European craftsmen. Our gracious home, with its blond-brick exterior, sat on a half acre of floodlit landscaping. Inside were hand-painted tiles and gleaming woodwork everywhere you looked. One of my favorite things was a built-in refrigerator detailed in blond wood with silver latch handles on each of the four doors. Cecil had his own apartment, a haven for his friends and growing collection of supercool jazz records. In addition to five bedrooms, Daddy had a pastor's study designed by an interior decorator from Robinson's Furniture on Washington Boulevard. It had a glossy mahogany desk and a high-back swivel chair, and his honors and awards lined the walls. That's where I sat almost nightly, talking to ardent admirers, heightening the romantic atmosphere by turning out the lights. Ah, those sweet teen years . . .

Daddy worked as much in his bedroom as in his study. That's where he would prepare his sermons and spend hours reading not only the Bible but serious studies of theology and history. As I've said, he never stopped learning, and he loved soul food. To break from his studies, he'd heat up some neck bones or black-eyed peas that our housekeeper and cook Katherine had prepared. We always knew when he was heating something up; the smell of those burnt skillets and pungent smoke drifted through the house.

On Sundays I tried to cook breakfast for Daddy. Katherine didn't work weekends, and I wanted him to have a good breakfast before church. When I started it took me two and a half hours to cook grits, ham, and eggs. When I reached his room with the tray, his worn-out, patient expression said everything. But he appreciated what I was trying to do and understood I had no experience cooking.

By then Erma had a baby boy herself. She was separated from her husband—they had lived briefly in Rockford, Illinois—and became a nurse's aide. So the house was filled with the sounds of cooing and crying, a little too much for Daddy, as noise carries upward. I remember him at the staircase yelling, "Aretha, will you get off the piano!" It was too early in the morning for musical appreciation.

Daddy had raised independent and ambitious daughters. Erma, Carolyn, and I all wanted musical careers. As he and my mother were great singers, it ran in the genes. Erma, though, would go on and graduate from college while her mother-in-law cared for her baby boy, Thomas Lee, Jr., and daughter, Sabrina. In the early sixties Erma would also go on the road with Lloyd Price, "Mr. Personality" the R&B star from New Orleans. For a while Erma went with Harold Logan, Lloyd's manager. I liked Logan. I remember him coming to Detroit to get Daddy's permission for Erma to travel. When the formalities were over and the discussion turned to business, Daddy asked, "What can you guarantee my daughter?" "I can't guarantee her anything," Logan replied. "Well, then, she can't go" was Daddy's firm stance. And Erma didn't—until a year later, when Daddy finally relented.

Earlier, while Cecil and Erma attended college in Atlanta, where

Erma also sang in a few local clubs, Carolyn was getting ready to go to Northwestern High. We were all leaving home or about to, and Daddy felt it was important for Carolyn to leave the nest as well. He arranged for her to stay with a family about two and a half blocks from our home. But Carolyn didn't understand this move to prepare her for independence. Without a mother or a woman's touch, it was difficult for both of them. I don't know what the conversation was between them, but it hurt Carolyn deeply. She felt abandoned and didn't understand the long-range benefits of Daddy's plan for her until we talked about it much later in California. Like the eagle that stirreth her nest, Daddy would have been there if Carolyn couldn't fly. But he knew that she could, and eventually she knew it too. Daddy loved us and would have killed a battalion for any one of us, especially the baby. Carolyn secured employment at the post office shortly thereafter and began writing legendary music, some of which I would later record.

After my second child, I did not return to high school. As my commitment to music deepened, the trips on the road with my dad got longer. Chess Records asked Daddy whether they could record me, and he agreed. My first record has been reissued in many versions and, I'm proud to say, is still available and played on many gospel programs, some four decades after I sang the sacred songs. Composed of nine numbers recorded live—some at New Bethel, some during out-of-town services—it reflects my musical inclinations and influences as a teenager.

Some of it was recorded at the Oakland Arena, scene of one of my fondest memories. The arena was spirit-filled as I sat at the piano and played and sang the Thomas A. Dorsey classic "Precious Lord." As singers say today, I was not singing that Sunday; I was "*saang*-ing." Later in my life "Precious Lord" was the one song that Dr. King always requested of me. My recorded version was done under the auspices of our promoters, the Reed Brothers. By then Daddy had become so popular that the civic auditorium was too small; that's how we wound up in the Arena.

Three of the songs on that album—"There Is a Fountain Filled with Blood," "The Day Is Past and Gone," and "While the Blood Runs Warm"—are associated with my mentor, Clara Ward. She and Daddy remained my dominant influences. "Never Grow Old" came from my childish infatuation with Billy Kyles of the Thompson Community Choir in Chicago. Billy was a close associate of Dr. King. In fact, moments before Dr. King was assassinated, Billy was a few feet from him. Dr. King was going to dinner at Billy's home.

Other songs on my debut album—"He Will Wash You Whiter Than Snow" and "Jesus Be a Fence Around Me"—were my first solos with the young adult choir. (And even earlier than that, at the old New Bethel, my first choice and favorite was "I Am Sealed.")

As our trips grew more extensive, the destinations became more exotic. Perhaps most exotic of all was Los Angeles. We went there several times yearly. It took three days, three nights, and the morning of a fourth day driving. Negotiating those narrow Rocky Mountain curves left me with big eyes. I had to hold my breath. But as a teenage girl, seeing and staying in black America's most fabulous hotels, I felt it was all worth it.

At the Watkins in Los Angeles, which served the best grits and sausages on the planet, I observed Nat "King" Cole seated in the lobby. In a herringbone hat, alpaca sweater, and sharp tailored slacks, he was the picture of class and elegance, relaxed, laid-back, and laughing with the boys. Nat Cole and my dad, both Aquarians, were similar in terms of class, sophistication, and confidence. His daughter Natalie has much to be proud of, as I do. (Speaking of Natalie, many years later I turned on *The Tonight Show* and heard her discussing her father. It encouraged me to open up and speak more about my dad. After he was shot in 1979, I was too hurt to speak about it for a very long time except to my family—and even then only briefly.)

After we performed in L.A., we went back to the hotel to relax for the evening. As I retired for bed, I turned on the radio to hear Dolphins of Hollywood playing Sam's new releases, "You Send Me," "Only Sixteen," and "For Sentimental Reasons (I Love You)" every few minutes. Sam's voice purred from the radio as I drifted off to sleep. (I thought that Sam had the only version of "For Sentimental Reasons" until I recently heard Nat "King" Cole's. Cole's rendition floored me. What a passionate, romantic, and sentimental reading! As a teenager I loved Sam's version; but as a mature woman I understood the depth of Cole's interpretation.)

L.A. also meant Heywood's Beauty and Barber Shop, where I'd go for the latest look. Frank McCray, famous as hairstylist to none other than the Godfather of Soul, James Brown, worked there. I also remembered that shop as a hotbed of fans of Smokin' Joe Frazier.

Our limousine service gave us the grand tour of Hollywood: the Brown Derby on Wilshire, Dino's on the Strip (with Dean Martin's face outlined in neon), Redd Foxx's nightclub, the Beverly Hills Hotel, those quaint fairy-tale homes and modern structures hanging off the sides of the Hollywood Hills on stilts. I loved smelling the sweet air while oohing and aahing at one beautiful estate after another.

Sam came over to the hotel and took us to his home, not far from the Watkins, where he gave me a beautiful suede jacket with fringes. It was better than new, because he had worn it. He brought out his guitar and performed some of his new material. J. W. Alexander, former member of the noted gospel group the Pilgrim Travelers and close friend to Sam, was also there. J.W. helped mold Sam's new pop career.

I deeply appreciated Sam's friendship. I am cognizant of the great friendships among artists—Chopin and Liszt, van Gogh and Gauguin, Tracy and Hepburn, or, for that matter, Daddy and Clara. When the egos of great artists can survive a friendship, friendship can be a beautiful happening between two people—supportive, enlightening, and enjoyable.

In my travels I had the opportunity to sing with the Caravans in Florida. I filled in because their newest member, Shirley Caesar, couldn't make it. What a super thrill! Naturally I knew all the parts from lying on the floor by the record player in the study listening to them for hours at a time. Later, by the way, Shirley followed the lead of the veteran Caravans Albertina Walker and Inez Andrews and became a major star in her own right.

Other gospel singers should have been bigger stars. Bessie Griffin, for example, was very underrated; she had the power to destroy an auditorium within seconds. Edna Gallmon Cooke was unique. These were ladies who sang with every fiber in their being. These were the exponents of what I now call traditional gospel. Stick-to-your-ribs gospel. Gospel performed by the giants—the Sensational Nightingales with Reverend Julius "June" Cheeks, the Gospel Harmonettes, led by Dorothy Love, fondly referred to as Dot, whom unfortunately I never had the occasion to meet.

My memory is alive with so many stirring performers "getting in the house," an expression we used long before the hip-hoppers: the Roberta Martin Singers, Gloria Griffin, who specialized in "God Specializes," Delois Barrett of the Barrett Sisters, with her million-dollar smile and roof-raising performances, the husband-wife duet Sullivan and Iola Lewis Pugh of the Consolers, and Maceo Woods with his incredible version of "Amazing Grace" on the Hammond organ.

The gospel circuit made me road savvy. After long drives I learned to hang my clothes in the bathroom, turn on the shower, steam out the wrinkles if I could not get pressing, and be ready for the early Sunday morning preservice broadcast.

The worlds of Gospel and pop were mutually appreciated; we were singing for the Lord and saving souls; stressing the message that said, For what does it profit a man to gain the whole world and lose his soul? Secular artists loved and respected us, knowing how, as Daddy once wrote, "Gospel music mends the broken heart, raises the bowed-down head, and gives hope to the weary traveler."

Daddy also understood the artistic value of secular music. He knew the day was arriving when my musical horizons would widen. Secular was an exciting prospect to me. The fifties were ending. In 1960 it was all about the nomination of John Kennedy to lead the Democratic Party as presidential candidate against Richard Nixon. Daddy was also excited about my prospects as a singer who could sing any kind of material. Before my eighteenth birthday, the path ahead seemed clear: I would test the waters and venture forth into the world of popular music. I would take a chance. If Sam could make it, perhaps I could too.

# The Big Apple

One of the first times I thought about going to New York alone or with a girlfriend involved the Flamingos. Both Erma and I had a thing for the Flamingos, the classiest and most professional of the doo-wop groups, the Four Tops of yesteryears.

I would daydream about flying to New York and then driving over to Wildwood, New Jersey, where the Flamingos were performing. I'd go so far as to call the airlines to check on flights. I had it all mapped out. But there was just one thing: I had no money, and I had never left home without my dad in my life.

In the fifties, through Harvey Fuqua, maestro of the Moonglows, I met Nate Nelson of the Flamingos. We dated. It wasn't a heavy affair; we went together only lightly and slightly, a whenever-I-see-you kind of thing, maybe once a year or so. In my most impressionable years, fine young crooners cast an especially romantic aura. One of the finest of all was Marvin Gaye, who was discovered by Fuqua. In fact, Marvin was in the last edition of the

Moonglows. When the group disbanded, he and Harvey headed to Detroit.

Harvey dated and later married Berry Gordy's sister Gwen, who actually founded a label before Motown. Harvey would bring Marvin by our house. Soon Marvin and Erma became an item. Marvin had an easy disposition, cool and beautiful, and sang with a tear in his voice. His romance with Erma didn't last long after she left for college. He wound up with Anna Gordy, another of Berry's sisters, who did much to promote Marvin's career.

When it came to my career, Daddy remained my chief adviser. As we approached my debut as a popular singer, I can recall one slight disagreement. A group of agents in Detroit wanted to sign me. Daddy urged me to go with them. But I wasn't comfortable with these people. I told my father that I preferred to keep looking. He took me outside in the hallway to talk to me, and I wound up getting slapped. However, I still refused to sign—thank God.

This is the time—1960—when Motown was starting up. They expressed interest in signing me, but both Daddy and I had our sights set on something bigger. At that time Motown was a fledgling local label. Little did we know that, in a few short years, they would be one of the great record companies of all time. Instead we concentrated on national and international labels, and that still pleases me today.

Before we arrived at Columbia, Daddy took me to New York to meet Phil Moore. Moore had helped some of the major stars of the day—Dorothy Dandridge and, most notably, Lena Horne. He was a master choreographer and arranger and, beyond that, a man who could create an overall image. He knew how to package and present artists. Daddy said Moore was the best and, for my about-to-be-born career, only the best would do.

By then I had begun singing songs like "Navajo Trail" (which I'd heard by Sam Cooke) and "Ac-Cent-Tchu-Ate the Positive." I sang a few of these numbers for Moore, remembering the melodies from Sam's records and adding my own vocal interpretations.

When I was through Daddy and I awaited the verdict. "Reverend," said Moore, "your daughter doesn't need big choreography. She doesn't need to be fluffed up or polished over with New York sophistication. I wouldn't touch or tamper with what she has naturally. She has a very special gift. Just let her do her thing and she'll be fine."

First thing we needed was a demo. Daddy recruited Major Holley, a superb bass player from Detroit who had longtime experience as a New York studio musician. Holley organized and supervised the session. I sang in front of a trio and, for the most part, the songs were standards like "My Funny Valentine" and Curtis Lewis's "Today I Sing the Blues." Lewis and Jo King, the woman who would soon become my manager, took the demo to John Hammond, a producer at Columbia, who contacted us almost immediately.

Later I learned that Sam Cooke was interested in getting me to sign at RCA, the label where he had enjoyed such crossover success. While Daddy and I were talking to Columbia, though, I never knew of Sam's interest. I have a feeling that if Sam had caught up with me, I would have gone to RCA. But it wasn't meant to be.

I can't remember the terms, but of course I remember John Hammond. We had been told that he had discovered Bessie Smith, Count Basie, and Billie Holiday. He praised me as having the best voice he had heard since Holiday, a tremendous compliment. In future years books would credit Hammond for discovering me, but it was Daddy who first realized my talent, and Daddy who first presented me to the public in gospel and prepared me for secular music with tender loving care.

I found Hammond approachable and supportive. He arranged my first session and provided me with the best studio musicians in New York. Later Hammond was kind enough to write of the first album, reissued as *The Great Aretha Franklin: The First 12 Sides*, "Aretha has all the passion of a gospel veteran, along with a humor and a natural vocal technique almost unknown in a jazz singer. This is the one album of Aretha's that has the feeling of jazz improvisation."

Ray Bryant was the piano player, Osie Johnson the drummer, Skeeter Best and Lord Westbrook on guitars, Milt Hinton and Bill Lee on bass, and Tyree Glenn on trombone. Hammond had confidence in me, inviting me to accompany myself on piano whenever it felt right. On songs like "Right Now" and "Maybe I'm a Fool," I did provide my own backing. By then I had a jazz-blues feel on piano that suited my vocal style, and, from time to time, I liked supporting myself. I also liked Ray Bryant, a brilliant jazz pianist who had a church background; Ray could play anything.

The tune I remember most vividly from those early sessions is "Today I Sing the Blues." Hammond remembered it as the first song sung at the first session, and he was right.

I also cut "Over the Rainbow," which had been a favorite of mine since I heard it done by Judy Garland. I didn't become a Judy fan until a little later, though as an adult I came to appreciate the depth of her soul and beauty of her interpretations. Today I consider her one of the supreme song stylists, whose ability to express emotion is without peer. Judy was a real diva.

The songs on these sessions were cut as singles—"Right Now," "It Ain't Necessarily So," "Who Needs You?" There was no thought of an album or album concept. As Hammond wrote, we were aiming for the "jukebox market." Columbia had been the leading label of the fifties with mainstream material, the home of

Mitch Miller, Leslie Uggams, and Johnny Mathis. Mahalia Jackson was also on Columbia; she was a great favorite of Goddard Lieberson, the head of the label, who sat in a big office upstairs and whom I never saw. In fact, for all my years at Columbia, I never saw Mahalia there. I did observe Connie Francis at 1650 Broadway before she became world-famous. And on occasion I would stop and chat with Leslie Uggams's mother, a lovely lady. We shared the same accountants, Lazaro & Company, on Fifty-seventh Street. I appreciated Leslie's recordings, particularly "The Eyes of God," and saw her as one of the early African American pioneers on Broadway.

If you listen to "Love Is the Only Thing," from one of my first sessions, you'll hear a male voice accompanying me. That's Paul Owens, who was a lead vocalist with the gospel group the Swan Silvertones, led by Claude Jeter and Louis Johnson. For a while Paul and I dated—more on that a little later. For the most part, though, my early years in New York were about working and moving forward, developing my career, classes, choreography, and rehearsals on Fifty-second Street and Broadway. It was all about trimming the baby fat.

Daddy continued to watch over me in the form of chaperones. I was happy when he sent Sue Dodds Banks to New York. Sue was a cool friend of my father and a driver for the McFall Funeral Home in Detroit. She had natural class and great taste in clothes. Sue knew her away around. When my wardrobe wasn't right, I'd borrow something from her. Sue had to-die-for pieces, exquisitely cut peignoirs from Paris and Rome. I was so deep into my career and concerned with gowns for the stage, I'd totally neglected my personal wardrobe.

Elizabeth Thornton, who had served as Mahalia's secretary, also traveled with me as chaperone. Her friends fondly called her Butch. Like Sue, Butch was a wonderful role model for a teenage girl encountering the ultrasophisticated world of New York for the first time.

I stayed all over the city. For a few weeks I lived at the YWCA before moving to the Bryant Hotel on Fifty-fourth and Broadway. And there was a period when I stayed at the Chelsea Hotel, the scene of an embarrassing episode. Inadvertently my father forgot to pay the weekly rent, and I was locked out of my room. My belongings were confiscated. I didn't mind that as much as the fact that they took my portable forty-five collection, including all my Sam Cooke singles and Billie Holiday records. But I let it all go; I never did go back to the hotel after getting my luggage.

I also stayed in Greenwich Village. I liked the artistic ambience, and I loved the fried perch in the small hotel off Washington Square where I lived for months at a time. By now you've surely noticed that good food has played a significant role in my life from day one, starting with Lola's homemade rolls and Big Mama's chicken and dumplings. Good cooks can simply blow your diet. We all love good food. But I wonder—had the cooks in my family been a little less talented, would I be dealing with the weight today?

Back in my early New York days, I dated one of the Midnighters, the group led by Hank Ballard. Most of the time, though, my life was low-key. With my sons back home under the capable care of Big Mama, I was a career girl trying to take a big bite out of the Big Apple.

I mentioned my first manager, Jo King, a Sicilian American with a peppery personality and aggressive attitude. Jo also managed the successful actor Brock Peters. She was the one who booked my first gigs in the small clubs of New York. She also wanted me to take finishing classes. To that end she hired a high-fashion model by the name of Petcy, who put me through the rigors of walking with a book atop my head. At first I thought that was interesting. After a while, though, I realized that wasn't me. "You should feel like you're floating," said Petey. "Fine," I replied, "but I'd rather walk than float."

I also had other classes, all of them in the midtown CBS building that was previously the Ed Sullivan Theater (now home of David Letterman). This was where all the aspiring performers—actors, singers, musicians, flamenco dancers, tap dancers, the whole spectrum of showbiz—rehearsed night and day on one of the six floors. Someone was doing something creative in every room. I loved hearing the rehearsal pianists and the rhythmic beats of the tap dancers. The building was bursting with energy and ambition. A man named Rudy was the manager and renter of rehearsal rooms; he had a mischievous twinkle in his eyes and a dry wit. Making life even juicier, the coffee shop downstairs served the best finger-licking cheeseburgers in all five boroughs.

For a short while I had a vocal coach, Miss Leola Carter, who introduced me to several useful techniques. One of her other students was the entertainer Larry Storch. My favorite instructor was the incomparable Cholly Atkins, master choreographer. Cholly had been half of the great dance team of Coles and Atkins and was considered the best in the business. I've always loved to dance, and Cholly was able not only to show me steps but to introduce me to the highly disciplined, highly structured art of stage movement. I loved getting into my tights and leotards and working with Cholly, who was later hired by Berry Gordy to groom the Motown acts.

Speaking of Motown, Berry's business had begun its big move. Of course I had known many of the Motowners from my childhood. I had seen Diana Ross, for example, once or twice around the neighborhood. We didn't develop a friendship, but early on I regarded her as a young professional and someone who worked hard to accomplish her goals. That was true of the whole Gordy operation. Smokey Robinson was another brilliant example. He had formed the Miracles and enjoyed a smash with "Shop Around." I particularly liked the early things he wrote for Mary Wells—"Two Lovers," "You Beat Me to the Punch," and "My Guy"—all of which had crossed over to the pop charts. I love Smokey, who reminds me of how far we both have come from Boston Boulevard and Belmont Street; my lifelong friendship with Smokey keeps me grounded.

In addition to Smokey, writer-producers like Holland-Dozier-Holland, Norman Whitfield, Mickey Stevenson, and Robert Bateman were stepping up to the plate and batting a thousand.

As for myself, I didn't have any hits, but I was being booked into the best clubs and getting good exposure. I was working steadily, although I wasn't making any money. Jo explained that after expenses there was nothing left. So I was still struggling, shopping at exclusive resale shops on Madison Avenue and bargain haunts like S. Klein on the Square. After my workouts and massages with Miss Mills, I was a beautiful size twelve; I would leave the spa feeling like a million dollars. I remember one night in particular coming out of the City Squire Hotel after a sauna treatment to a balmy seventy-five-degree evening; the combination of the weather and the massage and the sauna was nirvana.

John Hammond continued as my producer on the early sessions. I've never been easy to categorize, nor do I like being categorized, but I suppose you could say my early style was a combination of blues, gospel-based jazz, and rhythm and blues. I've always loved standards, so singing songs like "Rock-A-Bye Your Baby with a Dixie Melody" and "How Deep Is the Ocean?" came naturally to me. One of my mentors, James Cleveland, wrote "Nobody Like

You," a beautiful bluesy number and an unusual secular composition from the multitalented King of Gospel. (We've all got a love
life.) Hammond saw me as a blues-jazz artist, and although he hired
Bob Mersey, whose arrangements I absolutely adored, Hammond
didn't seem interested in pop hits. Personally, I was simply happy to
have a contract with a major company. I was also thrilled with the
high level of musicianship surrounding me. Hammond—and, for
that matter, everyone I worked with at Columbia—recruited the
best studio players and background singers around.

When friends like the Four Tops—Levi Stubbs, Obie Benson,
Duke Fakir, and Lawrence Payton—played the Apollo, I made it
my business to run up to Harlem to hear them. I myself couldn't
play the Apollo because I didn't have any hits. My show was tailored to jazz clubs and one-night venues. I felt it important to sing
songs people knew and could sing along with.

In the early sixties, when I heard Sam Cooke was in the city, I
called him. He was staying at the Warwick Hotel, just off Sixth Avenue in midtown (where, incidentally, two of the most beautiful
coats I've ever owned were stolen). He invited me over, and I
stopped by sooner rather than later. As I walked down the hallway
toward his room, I saw a woman coming out. She didn't see me,
but I recognized her profile, and it was the profile of a major star.
As a matter of privacy, I will withhold her name. I concluded later,
however, that she and I had similar good taste in men. Sam and I
had a lovely time chatting. He was his usual charming self, expressing interest in my career. I was always flattered by Sam's concern.

As a nightclub performer, I am mindful of the pioneering
women who preceded me, like Dinah Washington, Sarah Vaughan,
Lena Horne, Ella Fitzgerald, Hazel Scott, Ruth Brown, Damita
Woods, and Joyce Bryant. They were highly respected vocalists

who understood the art of elegant presentation. Of my generation, Nancy Wilson and others became stars in that same classy mode, opening major doors and leaving the buyers and promoters with the unmistakable impression that the African American chanteuse was responsible, qualified, and fabulous. I remember Nancy and Sid McCoy, a noted jazz deejay who loved himself some Nancy Wilson, both stopping by to see me at the Playboy Club in Chicago when it first opened. That's when the Golden Key Club had begun and the bunnies were the talk of the town and the country.

Looking back, I see that I was also developing a vocal signature. It wasn't anything I did consciously. And it wasn't part of a plan. It was simply me. As I branched out and sang different kinds of songs, the signature became apparent. Writers recognized this. Even hard-boiled jazz critics like Leonard Feather had important things to say about me. And for a young artist, critical accolades were extremely significant—even more so because, for all the praise, I still wasn't recording hits.

# The Circuit

For a long while I had a trio and sang jazz-tinged standards, covered some hit songs of the day, and interpreted bluesy ballads. At various times Ray Bryant, Teddy Harris, and Ellis Larkins accompanied me on piano. These men were distinct stylists and major artists in their own right. They helped my transition into the art of intimate nightclub singing.

Other singers working in this vein impressed me. Nina Simone and Betty Carter were wonderful, with unique attitudes and strong personalities. I also loved Andy Bey. Andy and the Bey Sisters worked the Village a great deal during my early years in New York. Soon as I finished my gig, I'd run over to hear them. Andy never got the recognition he deserved. He and his singing sisters were jazz originals and brilliant impressionists. So were Blossom Dearie and Peggy Lee. These ladies were hip; they knew how to entertain and stay true to their jazzy roots.

I appreciated many pop vocalists. Rosemary Clooney was cool, and so was Doris Day. I always thought Doris was underrated as a vocalist. I also loved her lighthearted movies and have always wanted to do films in the vein of *Pillow Talk* and *Where Were You When the Lights Went Out?* That was Doris at her comedic best. Her son Terry Melcher was at Columbia during my stint here, and we briefly met.

I was enjoying the road. And I was lucky that Granville White, the promotion man from Columbia, accompanied me to those early gigs. He and Deke, a promo man in Chicago, took me around to the radio stations to meet the jocks. Granville was a dapper gentleman who wore banker's pin-striped suits and comported himself like a polished pro. God bless Granny, who has since passed on.

I played the Tradewinds on Rush Street in Chicago. That's where I opened for Buddy Hackett. Buddy was wild, cracking up the crowd with his Chinese waiter routine. He was a big-time Hollywood star, the crème de la crème of Vegas and the Catskills Borscht Belt.

Opening for Buddy—at least my first night—was surprising. While I was rehearsing I heard a voice from the back yell, "Put some makeup on that girl!" It was the owner. He wanted my features to be more defined. Coming from the church, I was reluctant; I was accustomed to very little makeup, only lipstick and a little pencil. But now I got the point: it was important to be seen from the last row in the room. Without makeup my features wouldn't read from far away. I was beginning to learn the ropes.

Chicago was also the home of my friends the Staples. I spent time at their home and enjoyed being with their mom, a lovely lady.

Chicago meant the Playboy Club, where I was happy to open for another comic I admired, Dick Gregory, a supersharp intellectual. The work was steady, and, in addition to the funnymen, the instrumentalists with whom I shared many bills were inspiring.

During my early trio days, modern jazz was going through a soul period, rediscovering its funky and churchy roots. I was part of that mix. I'm talking about monster musicians like Freddie Hubbard and Blue Mitchell and Junior Mance. I was privileged to play dates at such a young age with the immortal John Coltrane. I observed Charlie Mingus slap one of his pianists onstage—I wasn't sure exactly why and couldn't believe my eyes—this was the same Mingus who played bebop with such fire and imagination. Audiences accepted me on bills with Art Blakey and the Jazz Messengers.

The Village Vanguard, perhaps the most prestigious jazz club in the world, booked me for months at a time. There was so much music coming out of the Vanguard you could hear it for blocks away. It was part of the appeal and charm of the Village of the early sixties. To get to my dressing room, I'd have to walk through the musicians' room. The fellows were hanging out and talking trash, but they were always cool and protective of me as I hurried through to get dressed. I can still see all the smoke and mirrors. And I can still see Professor Erwin Corey's disheveled hair and that infamous black tuxedo he wore with sneakers; I opened for him as well.

The La Carousel Club in Atlanta must go into the Guinness Book of Records as having the smallest dressing room on the planet, so small, in fact, that both feet couldn't fit inside. I swear to you, there was just a chair and a mirror and a curtain. If I put my foot a few inches to the right, I was out of the dressing room. I *have* paid my dues. What they lacked in dressing facilities, though, they made up for in food.

The highlights of this period were the dates I shared with mild-mannered Horace Silver, whose brand of piano jazz was right up my alley. Horace had his own style of funk. I loved to hear him rock the house with "Sister Sadie" and "Señor Blues."

At the same time I was playing jazz clubs and meeting jazz greats, I had the chance to make two long tours on the rhythm and blues circuit—one headlined by Sam Cooke, the other by Jackie Wilson. Each involved some twenty-eight one-nighters. These were the first and last tours I ever made. Some performers are meant to tour, but not me. The grind is much too much. After being in a different city every day, it got to the point where I didn't know if I was coming or going.

Back then, though, I was eager to go the distance and had no idea it was going to be so rough. Besides, who could resist touring with Sam and Jackie? They were consummate performers and serious eye candy. I adored them both, and they kind of liked me too.

Sam's tour was fabulous. Also featured were Sugar Pie DeSanto and Huey "Piano" Smith and the Clowns from New Orleans. At the start of the tour, I was still learning. I hadn't been out of gospel and Detroit for that long. We arrived at a civic auditorium and were escorted to one large dressing room. I had my one little green gown and also my chaperone, Sue Dodds Banks. "Okay," said Sam, "time to change and get dressed." Everyone started undressing, right then and there.

I was shocked and in a quandary. What to do? I just stood there pondering the situation, holding my gown, my eyes getting bigger by the moment. Sam saw what was happening. He looked up at me as if to say, *Come on, Ree . . . What's wrong, Ree?* When I didn't respond, he finally smiled. Then, demonstrating his charm as a gentleman, he took some boards, threw some clothes over them, and created a makeshift partition. During that tour, Sam's head was buried in *The Rise and Fall of the Third Reich,* and I decided I needed to investigate it too. I bought it and never read one page.

Jackie Wilson was supersmooth. He was from Detroit, and he and my brothers, Vaughn and Cecil, were good friends. Jackie always treated me with tender loving care. He was the man who introduced me to limousines, and I've been riding in them ever since. Limos give you that extra room that an artist needs after a long day. With a few pillows, you can turn the back of a limo into a bed if necessary. Jackie and I were riding on a cloud in one of his sleek long, black limos.

A former Golden Gloves champion, Jackie was quick with his hands and was absolutely devastating; he was one of the prototypes of a lady's and a man's man. He had a serious rep. I remember walking down Broadway with an associate of Jackie. I stopped to admire a beautiful pink silk dress I saw in a store window. Later I was gifted with said dress and, to put it mildly, was floored.

Beyond his personal style, Jackie was the performer's performer. He was doing it when no one else was doing it, and showing you how it was supposed to be done. I loved the way he backed onstage and spun around with his arms up, dropping to his knees with no sweat.

As I said, since those experiences, my performance bookings have been far more selective. But none of us could afford to be selective in the early days, when one night I might have been booked into a sophisticated jazz club, the next a funky lounge on the chitlin' circuit, and the third a teen hop. I've played my share of hops. The first was with Windsor King and the Cashmeres, appearing with the memorable Baby Washington. The Cashmeres were a cool Frankie Avalon–style act and, for a while, Windsor and I were close friends. For someone so young, Windsor had impressive business skills.

Back on the jazz circuit, I worked the Showboat Club in Philly and was thrilled to see Clara Ward in the audience. It did my heart good to know there were gospel stars confident enough as Christians to support me at a nightclub. Clara knew who she was and

thought nothing of sipping a ginger ale while enjoying my performance. Les McCann, whose piano artistry came straight from the
soul, frequently performed at the Showboat, alternating with me.
And there was the Philadelphian Bill Cosby, who came in the early
days to hear me at the Cadillac Club on Broadway Street. I enjoyed
his support and have always appreciated and loved him as a comedian, humanitarian, teacher, and friend.

I met Miles Davis in Philly. He, Patti LaBelle, and I shared a bill
at the Uptown Theater. I remember my chaperone, Sue, and me
laughing about Miles's green trumpet. I also recall him trying to
corner me and buss me, but it never came off. It wasn't a heavy
thing, just Miles being Miles.

When I first saw Dionne Warwick, we were both barely out of
our teens. She had just recorded "Walk On By." I heard this melody
playing on the radio and turned it up, saying to myself, *Who is this?*
*I really like this.* Subsequently, she and I played one or two of the
same teen hops. Dionne had confidence, poise, and a unique style.
She is another artist who made a graceful segue from gospel to pop
and racked up many memorable classics. Some of my favorites are
"Don't Make Me Over," "Walk On By," "Anyone Who Had a
Heart," and "Valley of the Dolls."

Over the years Dionne and I have made the effort to support
each other with various charities and civic fund-raisers. We also
share a passion for interior decoration. Along with Roberta Flack
and Nancy Wilson, Dionne has proved to be one of the more mature women in the business, who didn't allow ego or insecurities
to short-circuit soliciting other artists for worthy causes.

Back in the early sixties, I played the Paradise Club in Idlewild,
Michigan, an exclusive African American resort where Daddy
Braggs, Della Reese's onetime sweetie, ran the show. The shows
were a must—a sepia version of the June Taylor Dancers, gorgeous

showgirls. Similar to Daddy Braggs's show was Larry Steele's Revue at Club Harlem in Atlantic City. I went there with my children Clarence and Eddie, and remember that the breakfast shows didn't start till midnight. I wouldn't be off until about 4:00 A.M., so I let the boys go over and visit with the showgirls, who fussed over them all evening and put them to bed while I was onstage. Atlantic City was a good time, especially those after-hours meals at Kelley's—hot-sauced wings and grits for days.

Back in the studio with Columbia, I was vacillating between material for adults and songs for teens. John Hammond was out of the picture after the first couple of sessions. I never knew why. Understand that I was still naïve about the business of the music industry. I was happy to have the opportunity to sing and responded positively to the songs and producers who came my way. I was down for the music and missed the political nuances; I was in my own world of music.

When Bob Mersey came along, for example, I saw him as a highly professional arranger who surrounded me with exceedingly lush sounds. And when I walked into the studio and heard his arrangement of my very first composition—"Without the One You Love"—all those strings playing my music, I was so touched it brought me to tears. Who needed money? That was my music playing!

To this day "Skylark," another Mersey arrangement, is one of my favorites. I sang any number of songs I loved—"Try a Little Tenderness," "For All We Know," "Make Someone Happy," and, from *Camelot,* which was all the rage in the early sixties, "If Ever I Would Leave You."

Naturally I was stunned by the news of Dinah Washington's death. She was the Queen. When she died in 1963 under tragic circumstances, we were all stunned. It was suggested that I sing a tribute. I was honored to be asked. *Unforgettable,* after her big hit, was the name of the album, and Bob Mersey wrote ten beautiful charts for ten songs I had selected.

As I sang, of course I thought about my brief personal association with Dinah in Detroit, those nights I heard about her walking the bar at the Flame Show Bar, people jammed in twenty deep and spilling out into the streets for blocks. I recalled catching a glimpse of her in Chicago, her hometown, as she sashayed across the parking lot on her way to the newly built Roberts Hotel; her short jacket was stylish and her hat broke beautifully. She was kind of sharp that night. Another time she came by my dressing room at a nightclub on the West Side of Detroit and commented that my shoes needed to be arranged in a more orderly fashion; many times I step out of things and leave them where they are until I return later to pick them up. My unspoken response was, *What does she have to do with my dressing room or the arrangement of my shoes?* However, I was highly flattered that the Queen had stopped by to hear me sing.

On the LP *Unforgettable* I sang one of Dinah's R&B songs—"Soulville." It marked my first experience with overdubbing, adding a number of voices, usually in harmony, to the main vocal. I believe I was among the first vocalists to implement this technique. All those years with James Cleveland gave me the confidence to create my own harmonies and backgrounds.

After my tribute to Dinah, Columbia decided to package me more commercially. They hired the producer Clyde Otis. In fact, Clyde had written and produced for Dinah for many years and enjoyed a long string of smashes; he understood the youth market. Clyde was a big man, warm and friendly, who worked hand-in-glove with the arranger Belford Hendricks, nicknamed Sinky. Our first effort to make any noise was "Runnin' Out of Fools," a funky little turntable hit. That meant strong radio play but only so-so sales. We also covered Dionne's "Walk On By" and a Motown hit by Brenda Holloway, "Every Little Bit Hurts," as well as the super-smash Smokey Robinson wrote and produced for Mary Wells, "My Guy." My version languished.

When I came home to be with my children and family, I'd occasionally run over to Motown on West Grand, my favorite boulevard, only a few blocks from our house on LaSalle. I'd peep into the studio to see who was cutting that day.

Berry Gordy won my respect with his aggressive business acumen and nice-guy manner. Mostly I admired his personalized attention to his artists. Detroiters were megaproud of Berry and Smokey and the Motown groups. Our local heroes and heroines were showing the world the talent of our beloved hometown. I wished them well yet have never regretted going a different route. I'm not sure I would have adjusted or adapted to their style. Fortunately, my own style continued to develop naturally on its own. Besides, Motown had a reputation for exercising complete control, and if so, it definitely would not have been the label for me.

Back in New York, getting booked on *The Ed Sullivan Show,* the biggest thing on TV, was a major move. We'd all grown up on Ed Sullivan. I was truly excited and set to sing two standards, the ballad "Skylark" and a brassy up-tempo "Moon River." Cholly Atkins and I had worked for months on this appearance. I was onstage, feeling especially good about my dress, a gorgeous silk gown with orange-gold beading made by Margaret Brown of Detroit, when out of the dark came a voice over the invisible loudspeakers: "Did Miss Franklin bring another gown? That one is too low-cut." Too low-cut? Well, this wasn't *Sesame Street.* I didn't understand the statement. In my opinion, the gown was modestly cut.

Fortunately, I *had* brought several other gowns and quickly changed. In my dressing room I waited. And waited. Then I was pulled aside by Joe Marsolais of Universal Attractions. He had something important to discuss. Could we step outside? "Aretha," he said, "I'm so sorry to say it, but you've been bumped off the show."

"What do you mean?" I asked. He explained that they had over-booked and someone had to be eliminated. I was stunned . . . blown away. As I walked back into the dressing room, tears welled up in my eyes.

In the light of records like "Soulville" and "Runnin' Out of Fools," I was booked on many of the teen TV shows. I did *Shindig* and *American Bandstand*. *American Bandstand* was especially cool. As a kid I had watched it and even knew the names of the regular dancers. Dick Clark turned out to be personable and kind. I liked him to begin with, and throughout my career he has never changed. Before that my first TV appearance was in Cleveland with Mike Douglas, another good guy.

Little by little, I was being exposed to the American public; slowly but surely, I was on my way.

# Young, Naïve, and Starry-Eyed

In 1960, just when my career was getting started and my focus shifted to New York, Detroit was undergoing major changes. For one thing, an urban renewal program meant the end of the New Bethel of my childhood. The Chrysler Freeway was being built right through Hastings. The church—in fact, the entire neighborhood—was being torn down for the highway. (Daddy spoke of how the Catholic church, only one block away, was saved from demolition while ours was not. He couldn't explain why.) Fortunately, I would get to perform at the neighborhood's most famous nightspot, the Flame Show Bar, before the end of its golden era. In fact, I seemed to perform at key nightspots—the Paradise in Idlewild, the Copacabana in New York, the Coconut Grove in L.A.—just before they closed. I wasn't twenty-one—I was barely eighteen—but rules were bent, and I sang at the club where Billie Holiday, Dinah Washington, T-Bone Walker, Sam Cooke, Arthur Prysock, and so many others had sung before me.

After several temporary quarters, among them Twelfth Street

and Seward, New Bethel moved from Hastings to the corner of Linwood and Philadelphia, refurbishing the old Oriole Theater, which seated some three thousand parishioners. That's where it remains today. Prophet Jones had preached at the Oriole for years. The new New Bethel was a suitably good setting for my father's growing popularity. But even now I feel the pull of those days in the old neighborhood down on Hastings, with the Willis Theater across the street, small shops and storefront churches as far as the eye could see.

The early sixties was a tumultuous time. In addition to the upheaval in so many American inner cities, what some called urban renewal was urban removal. The civil rights movement was in full swing. My father was an important and significant force in the movement. In fact, Daddy organized and led the historic march in Detroit in 1963 along with Dr. Martin Luther King, Ben McFall, Del Rio, and other notable Detroiters. Some 200,000 people marched. Many saw the event as the model for the March on Washington, which would come only two months later. Dr. King himself came to Detroit and gave the same speech, "I Have a Dream," that he delivered in the nation's capital.

Dr. King was a close family friend, a fabulous human being, a warm and shining example of humanitarianism and courage. After hearing about the civil rights movement and seeing it on TV, I asked my father's permission to participate. Daddy was proud to have me appear with Dr. King on four occasions, singing at money-raising concerts for the cause. I recall Harry Belafonte, Andrew Young, Bernard Lee, and the singer Esther Morrow participating in some of these events.

At one of the events our commitment was tested by a bomb scare. I had just finished singing when the sound of an enormous explosion shook the room. We ran for cover, not knowing what had happened. Fortunately, no one was hurt.

Daddy also preached in 1968 at the Poor People's March in Washington. His political and civic commitment was unwavering. He would often invite speakers like Adam Clayton Powell to address the church on issues that had special impact on the lives of black Americans.

The political upheavals of the early sixties had an impact on us all. On November 22, 1963, I was in the Broadway Market in downtown Detroit, a popular gourmet emporium, standing among hanging salamis and various spices and hams. On that afternoon and at that moment, the world was all about the pungent aromas of good food. Then someone said the president had been shot. People starting rushing around the market. Radios began to get louder. People gathered in groups on the streets. Suddenly the terrible news was in the air. President Kennedy was dead. We all walked out of the market and stood on Broadway talking about it. The president was so appreciated and loved by the African American community. I felt sad and hurt for the country—and particularly for his family.

I was focused on work. I mentioned that when I first arrived in New York, I briefly dated Paul Owens of the Swan Silvertones. That relationship, though, was short-lived. We were going out of town, and I stopped to pick him up at this hotel. When I arrived, he wasn't waiting downstairs. After a half hour or so in the car, I went to check on him. *Big mistake.* They didn't have the one-way see-your-guest peepholes in the doors in those days. When he opened the door and saw me he was blown away, and immediately put his arm across the door. I turned around and walked away without saying anything; all was obvious. *I'll be damned,* I thought. *How could he?*

About half an hour later he came downstairs, got in the car, and we started on our way to someplace in the South. After a long spell of blessed silence, all hell broke loose. We had a verbal and bit of a slapping and pushing scenario. Later I understood my father told him, "You had better back off and leave my daughter alone because you know you are not cool." That was the end of my brief fling with Paul.

A little later I was at a club in Brooklyn when I saw a singer take the stage and kill B. B. King's "Sweet Sixteen." *Who is this fine young brother turning it out?* I asked myself. The answer was Ronnie Isley.

Our friendship was tested, though, when he and his brothers invited Erma and me to a party at their house in the New Jersey suburbs at which there were no other guests or food. I was ready to leave. We decided there was no party here and we sure weren't going to *be* the party. When we asked them to take us home, though, their response was somewhat vague. Erma and I had to walk a mile down a dark country path to find a cabstand. Needless to say, we were never guests of the Isleys again. Many years later, however, they and I had a big laugh about it, and we remain friends today.

After moving to New York, I came home regularly. With all my choreography classes, my vocal lessons, and successful engagements in name nightclubs, I considered myself something of a star. Now, in retrospect, I see I was too young to know the true meaning of the term, but you couldn't tell me that then. It wasn't that I was arrogant, but I did feel above certain tasks. Housekeeping was far too mundane for me. Did I need someone to keep my feet on the ground and my head out of the clouds? Absolutely.

Daddy swiftly brought me back down to earth by telling me to introduce myself to the sink full of dirty dishes. When I finished that, I could mop the kitchen floor. My star was descending. Daddy taught me to maintain balance and not let accolades swell my head.

It was on one of these trips back to Detroit that, through my sister Erma, I met Ted White. I recalled she had a long conversation with a man on the telephone out on our sunporch. I asked her who she was talking to, and she replied, "Ted White." She also said he considered me among the most beautiful women in the world. One thing led to another, and before you knew it he was calling me. Still being extremely inexperienced and sheltered, I didn't realize I was in way over my head. It crossed my mind that he was the man I had seen carrying Dinah Washington out of the house years before.

It was the era of after-hours clubs in Detroit. And White introduced me to them. By then the Twenty Grand had replaced the Flame Show Bar as the hot place for the in crowd. Motown acts were often featured there. It was at the Twenty Grand that I first met the supersuave Four Tops. Their lead singer, Levi Stubbs, and Cecil were great friends. Soon I developed a lifelong friendship with the fellows as well. We all loved the Temptations, too (and I will detail my involvement with one Temp in particular a little later on)—we appreciated all the great lead Temps, from David Ruffin on—but the Tops hold a special place in my heart.

Detroit was a happening town in the sixties, and I was happy to come home and be part of the mix. Ted White knew his way around this new Detroit. He was a take-charge kind of guy, and before I knew it he had become my manager. I thought he had style and confidence. He also appreciated sophisticated jazz greats, like Dinah and Sarah. We started to date.

White formulated a new trio for me—Teddy Harris on piano,

Hindell Butts on drums, and Roderick Hicks on bass. Later he hired Donald Townes as my conductor. A gifted Detroit pianist, Earl Van Dyke, accompanied me for several years. Earl was a founding member of the Funk Brothers, the rhythm section that backed many of Motown's biggest hits.

My career was progressing slowly, and at one point White went to the pawnshop for additional money. He was seeing young ladies other than myself, yet oddly enough peace prevailed. (How naïve can you be?) On other occasions, however, things got out of hand; alcohol played a destructive role. Drinking ultimately damaged, and finally destroyed, our relationship.

Before all that, though, we were married by a justice of the peace on the road somewhere in Ohio and went for dinner afterward. I don't recall why I was not married in New Bethel with Daddy presiding. Somehow the idea of having a big church wedding with my father present was never discussed. Our marriage, as I recall, was the result of White's spontaneous suggestion. At some point he opened a small office in downtown Detroit on Broadway and represented a few songwriters—Mack Rice, James Epps, a talented duo by the name of Tony and Tyrone, and Ronnie Shannon. In a few years Shannon would make major contributions to my career.

By the mid-sixties I was pregnant and in Los Angeles at the Knickerbocker Hotel, where I discovered Russian dressing (the best thing since cheeseburgers—do you think I should have gone into the food business?), and I was working the 5-4 Ballroom, the spot for R&B lovers. On this particular night I shared the bill with the romping stomping Ike and Tina Turner. Tina wore a beautiful outfit with a flop hat that complemented the rest of her wardrobe. We all shared a dressing room, but we were never in it at the same time and never spoke to each other during the engagement. I felt particularly pleased with my gown, a long, white, two-piece creation with a subtle flare that gracefully camouflaged my pregnancy.

The problem, though, was that Tina and the Ikettes had funked so hard that dust was flying everywhere. They were doing their funky routines with the hair flying and the butts shaking. I mean, the dust was so thick you couldn't see a foot in front of you. Throwing down. When it was my turn, I decided to wait ten minutes or so until it had all settled. The evening turned out in a throw-down. "Today I Sing the Blues" and "Won't Be Long" were the highlights of my performance.

A couple months after the 5-4 Ballroom and Ike and Tina, my third son, Teddy, came into the world, and like all my children, he was a beautiful infant with the sweetest smile. He loved bananas, but they didn't love him; he threw them up on me and, to get out of the way of the spray, I had to move superfast. Several times while I changed his diapers, he would get me right up front.

❧

I was stunned by the death of Sam Cooke in December 1964. I was in Cleveland when Daddy called me. Before he gave me the tragic news, he asked if I was sitting. Then he said it plainly: Sam had been shot in L.A. Sam was gone. I couldn't believe it, yet it was true. It was my father speaking to me. I remember speaking to J. W. Alexander, who relayed some of the details. The fact was that a great artist, great man, and good friend was gone at the age of thirty-three. Sam will always be remembered and celebrated; his music lives on in the hearts and souls of fans from generation to generation. I look back and fondly treasure the moments I spent with him.

By this time, still in my early twenties, I had established a national reputation. You couldn't call me a star, but I was surely a working singer. I didn't have any real hits, yet Columbia continued picking up my options. They believed in me. Perhaps because they respected my artistry, or because they believed my breakthrough hit was only a record away, they never dropped me. So I was out there on the jazz-club circuit one day and the R&B circuit the next.

I played venues like the Regal in Chicago, where I was so happy that Lola came to see me. I also recall a food stand, tucked a few doors away from the theater, that served greasy burgers made with a spicy sausage in the meat, topped with crispy fries. Lord, have mercy. The artists couldn't wait to get offstage to wolf down those burgers. The show at the Regal was just as good—me, the Contours, the Marvelettes, the Temptations, Gene Chandler, and McKinley Mitchell. There were also club dates with the fabulous Cannonball Adderley, whose melodic approach created the kind of jazz I loved best. In both worlds, jazz and R&B, I consistently got good reviews.

Even though my base was New York, I stayed close to my family. My relationship with Ted White was educational to say the least. He continued as my manager. For better or for worse, my life had a rhythm. I recorded, I performed, I came home to see my father and my children. I stayed focused on my career. By 1967 I had been at the job of singing secular music for seven years. I was twenty-five. I was in it for the long haul and, by then, not expecting any miracles. You can imagine my surprise when, in very short order, a miracle did occur. My career exploded.

# The Breakthrough

I believe it was fate.

Fate brought me to Atlantic Records, where all the elements were right. Atlantic was the home of some of my favorite childhood artists—Ruth Brown, Ray Charles, Clyde McPhatter and the Drifters, the Clovers. It was the winter of 1966 when I switched from Columbia to Atlantic.

I felt a natural affinity with the Atlantic sound. To me, Atlantic meant soul. And more and more—especially with the advent of Atlantic artists like the Young Rascals, Arthur Conley, and Wilson Pickett—soul music was exploding. Stax was a subsidiary of Atlantic and had a heavy soul roster—Isaac Hayes, Sam and Dave, Otis Redding, and Eddie Floyd. A new wave of blues-based soul was sweeping the country.

Word went out that my Columbia contract was up, and Jerry Wexler, an Atlantic owner, got in touch with Ted White. The conduit may have been my gospel deejay friend Louise Bishop, the wife of Jimmy Bishop, also a popular deejay out of Philadelphia. In those days Louise was somewhere in the mix.

White and I went to New York, where Wexler offered me a thirty-thousand-dollar signing bonus. I accepted. With all the fine records I had made at Columbia, I wasn't sure how I would like Atlantic, but I was willing to try. I wanted a hit, and I wanted to be with a company that understood the current market.

Right from the start, I felt good about the arrangement. Columbia was a giant corporation. Columbia had surrounded me with the finest musicians, but it was somewhat impersonal. Atlantic was just the opposite. Jerry Wexler was warm and personal. He invited me to his home in Great Neck, where I met his children and his wife, Shirley. I spent several long evenings out there listening to records and looking for material. It was evident that Jerry had the preparation. What's more, he was interested in getting my input and approval on everything.

Jerry had a different approach. He wanted to base the music around me, not only my feeling for the song but my piano playing and basic rhythm arrangement, my overall concept. Until the Sweet Inspirations came onboard, I did all of the backgrounds, either alone or with my sister Carolyn. Occasionally my cousin Brenda helped with a few backgrounds as well. I liked this.

My years at Columbia had served as a wonderful workshop in which I observed the basics of studio production. Now Jerry handled all the technical aspects and made sure I put my personal stamp on these songs. Atlantic provided TLC—tender loving care—in a way that made me feel secure and comfortable. I went to work.

For the first session, Jerry wanted me to go to Muscle Shoals, where he had found, as he put it, "a rhythm section of Alabama white boys who took a left turn at the blues." White and I went down there and discovered great musicians who were good and funky, guys like Spooner Oldham, Jimmy Johnson, Roger Hawkins, David Hood, and Tommy Cogbill. I had worked out the approach to a song called "I Never Loved a Man (the Way I Love You)" by Ronnie Shannon, one of the Detroit writers represented by White. Spooner Oldham played beautiful electric piano lines while I was on acoustic. That's another key difference between my Columbia and Atlantic sessions. Putting me back on piano helped Aretha-ize the new music.

Many of the arrangements were done on the spot, in what we called head sessions. This was worlds away from how I had worked at Columbia, far more spontaneous and free-flowing, with so much more room to be creative. When we had the song on tape, the musicians and the arranger, Arif Mardin, and Jerry and I were ecstatic. We would all listen intently over the big speakers in the studio and sometimes would go in the control booth, where the smaller speakers projected what it would sound like on the radio. The enthusiasm and camaraderie in the studio were terrific, like nothing I had experienced at Columbia. This new Aretha music was raw and real and so much more myself. *I loved it!*

There has been speculation concerning a big confrontation in Muscle Shoals between Ted White and one of the musicians. It's been so long and so many things have happened since those days, I really don't recall. I do remember, however, some kind of friction, and I do remember White going upstairs to discuss something, but he never came back. I vaguely recall loud noises and voices shouting and doors slamming. I never learned the details. I was uncomfortable enough, though, that I decided to leave. The next morning I went to the airport alone. As soon as I got there, I ran into White.

Obviously he was leaving without me, and I without him. We flew back to New York together, with neither of us saying anything about the previous night.

Back in New York, there was no difficulty in the Atlantic studios. Jerry sent for the boys from Muscle Shoals, and we threw down. In addition to Jerry expertly handling the technical aspects, he brought in two other team members who, for years to come, would provide the perfect complement to our efforts. Tommy Dowd was the engineer of engineers, a genius behind the boards. And Arif Mardin was a musician's musician; whether it was horn charts or string charts, Arif had the magic touch, illustrious arrangements of depth and beauty. The results are a credit to the sensitivity of Jerry, Arif, and Tommy.

The pattern set on my first Atlantic album, named after the first single, "I Never Loved a Man (the Way I Love You)," would become the model for most of my Atlantic work to follow. With Jerry's help, I selected the songs. I also wrote many of them. At Columbia I had written only sporadically. Back in the early sixties, I had sold my publishing rights to Aaron Shroeder for a few hundred dollars, trying to earn my own money without consulting my dad. Being a novice, I didn't know any better. I didn't really understand the mechanics of the music and didn't really care to. As a young woman, I was into music and music only. My favorite place was the studio.

By the time I signed with Atlantic, I hadn't yet mastered the essentials of the business; it was still Greek to me. My attitude was, *Do I really have to sit and listen to all of this? Let's get to the music.*

On that first album, I contributed "Dr. Feelgood (Love Is a Serious Business)." White wrote a few of the lyrics here and there, but the majority of my songs came from my heart and soul and were created solely by me. Carolyn and I wrote "Baby, Baby, Baby" back in Detroit when I had a place on Fourteenth Street. King Curtis, the sax man who would soon become my musical director, wrote "Save Me," and, being a generous gentleman, gave Carolyn and me credit for our minor contributions. King was on staff at Atlantic and another significant influence on some of my early recordings. His "Soul Serenade," also on my Atlantic debut, is one of my all-time favorites. I also included "Drown in My Own Tears" because I loved Ray Charles's original version so much.

"Respect," of course, was a recent Otis Redding song. Carolyn and I coined the phrase "Sock it to me, sock it to me, sock it to me" in the middle of "Respect." It became a household expression through the recording industry and the TV program *Laugh-In,* and we never got a dime of credit. "Do Right Woman—Do Right Man," by Dan Penn and Chips Moman, came in through Jerry Wexler.

Look over the selections on this first album, and you see that soul was the key. There was no compromising, no deliberate decision to go pop. As it turned out, these records crossed over and sold on the charts. But we weren't trying to manipulate or execute any marketing plan. We were simply trying to compose real music from my heart.

As much as I appreciate the soulful studio environment in which Atlantic placed me and the sensitive musicians who played by my side, one point was deceptive and unfair: I was not listed as a co-producer. Wexler was the producer, and later Dowd and Mardin were coproducers. Looking back, I see that I certainly fulfilled a co-producer's role. At the time I didn't realize the crucial significance of my function. And in the music business few people tell you anything, particularly if you don't ask. No one volunteers pertinent information.

I was so thrilled by making the music that, once again, I neglected the business side. Producer credit and publishing shares seemed like minor details. I was the artist, and I was already getting my writer's credits, so at twenty-five I still had a lot to learn. Bored at business meetings, I'd actually go to sleep. Little did I know how much money was going back and forth across the table until my awakening. Then I decided I would get into the business of it.

The important thing going through my mind was that my single on Atlantic, "I Never Loved a Man (the Way I Love You)," took off like a rocket. What a moment! No wonder I wasn't concerned about coproducer credit. I had just had my first million-seller, and I felt like a million myself. After so many hitless years with Columbia, my dream was coming true.

"Respect" turned out to be an even bigger hit. It is still my biggest song in concert today. So many people identified with and related to "Respect." It was the need of a nation, the need of the average man and woman in the street, the businessman, the mother, the fireman, the teacher—everyone wanted respect. It was also one of the battle cries of the civil rights movement. The song took on monumental significance. It became the "Respect" women expected from men and men expected from women, the inherent right of all human beings. Three decades later I am unable to give a concert without my fans demanding that same "Respect" from me. "Respect" was—and is—an ongoing blessing in my life.

In another vein, "Dr. Feelgood" also proved enormously popular. I wrote it as an updated version of the blues, with the age-old wisdom that a good woman needs a good man—the same wisdom, by the way, that informs "Do Right Woman—Do Right Man."

Everything about that first Atlantic album pleased me—the acceptance, the sales, the musical power, the cover design, in which I wore a paillette-covered jumpsuit. Paillettes are decorative circles of see-through plastic, which, taken from my jumpsuit, were also fashioned into matching earrings. They remind me of fish scales.

As my records proved increasingly popular, the demand for my performances skyrocketed. Fashion became important to me, but it always had been. Just as I was determined to maintain a high level of excellence in my music, I wanted thoughtfulness reflected in my stage apparel. I had finally reached the plateau where I was being called a star.

The events of this breakthrough period came at a dizzying pace. My career exploded, just as the country itself was exploding with protests against the Vietnam War. The civil rights revolution was at its height. It was neither my intention nor my plan, but some were saying that in my voice they heard the sound of confidence and self-assurance; they heard the proud history of a people who had been struggling for centuries. I took these compliments to heart and felt deeply humbled and honored by them. Critics from *Playboy* to *Billboard* were naming me Female Singer of the Year. The accolades were pouring in. Who wouldn't have been jumping for joy?

But there was no time to bask in glory. Nowadays, artists may release a record every three or four years. Back then it was every five or six months. *I Never Loved a Man (the Way I Love You)* was released in March 1967; by early August of the same year, *Aretha Arrives,* with no fewer than eleven fresh songs, arrived in stores. One of those songs, "Baby, I Love You," another Ronnie Shannon creation, became another million-seller.

Because I was so hot, promoters were calling to book me everywhere. I was offered long tours and appearances in the most exclusive rooms in the world—Las Vegas, Atlantic City, Europe, South America, the Caribbean, you name it. But I quickly realized that I was the one who would be doing most of the preparation and work. It was my name and reputation out front. I was the one in concert, and soon I became the one who would have final say about what I would and would not do. In my opinion, no one was really looking out for me except my brother Cecil. The attitude was, Hey, let's get it while it's hot, with no thought of the pressure on me. My two previous tours—with Sam Cooke and Jackie Wilson—had not left my memory. I agreed to select dates, insisting that I would not abuse my voice or myself for anyone, a policy I honor to this day.

I was introduced to Ruth Bowen at Queen Booking through Ted White. Her agency had been named after Dinah Washington, Ruthie's longtime associate and friend. Ruthie was a pioneer in booking black entertainment, a very classy and savvy businesswoman. We became very close friends. We have had some differences over the years, but we have weathered the storms and maintained our friendship.

Larue Mann, Ruthie's close friend and confidante, became my wardrobe mistress and friend, traveling with me to all concerts, caring for the wardrobe, sewing, and giving attention to every imaginable detail.

My exposure was widening. I appeared on *The Tonight Show* with Johnny Carson. Harry Belafonte and Lena Horne were there to cheer me on. How stunning, and what a tremendous gesture by two of the legendary names in the business! And for the first time I began to headline at venues like the Regal in Chicago, the Howard in Washington, and the Uptown in Philadelphia. I watched other artists from the wings. I still fondly recall Billy Stewart singing "Summertime" and Chuck Jackson belting out "Any Day Now." Gene Chandler was also on those shows. Gene was not only the Duke of Earl, he was the knockout man in a toe-to-toe confrontation early one morning in my dressing room, before I got there. Upon opening the door, I saw that half of the mirror had been broken. *What on earth has been going on in here?*

On the strength of my early Atlantic hits, I could finally play the Apollo. The Apollo was always jumping. There was Count Basie, tying up the backstage phone while placing his horse and number bets; and there was Redd Foxx, patiently teaching me how to take full bows like a lady. What a place—up and down two or three flights of stairs four or five times a day, running around the corner in front of the theater for charcoal-broiled steaks between shows, and all those burgers, milk shakes, and fries backstage. Excitement and love were in the air.

Some of my glorious memories of the sixties, though, aren't all about me, they're about my dad. My father's fame continued to spread. He had reached a point of prominence where even the Apollo asked him to appear. Doing so, though, would mean cutting his sermons, and that, he felt, would be compromising the message. Beyond that, performing at the Apollo would entail five or six shows a day. The strain on his voice would be too much. So he declined.

I look back and fondly remember the days Daddy was honored at anniversary dinners at swanky downtown Detroit hotels. These were splendid occasions, when the ladies of the church would be dressed to the nines. The mayor of the city would always attend, and usually our congressmen and senators as well. It was also a chance for Daddy's three daughters to demonstrate our love for him by singing as a trio. Cecil was standing by and assisting Daddy, and Vaughn had gone to Vietnam. I vividly recall the anniversary dinner at which Erma, Carolyn, and I sang smooth three-part harmony on "Hush . . . Hush, Sweet Charlotte"—from the Bette Davis movie—along with "Dear Heart" and Jr. Walker's "Shotgun."

On "Shotgun" I played piano and sang the lead. Carolyn took off and did a dance that had everyone on their feet screaming.

Back in the studio, we kept the heat on high. On my second Atlantic effort, *Aretha Arrives,* I alternated background singers. On some songs I used Carolyn and Erma. There was nothing like the satisfaction of singing with my sisters and cousin Brenda. We were always in sync and had a very distinctive and family sound.

I had known Cissy Houston and her cousin Dee Dee Warwick at Columbia. At Atlantic, the Sweet Inspirations, who made such a sweet contribution to my sound, were now Cissy, Myrna Smith, Sylvia Shemwell, and Estelle Brown. For a brief period Estelle sang background with me. In most instances the Inspirations created the backgrounds. If I had one or two parts I wanted them to sing, I would tell Cissy, who would implement the harmonies.

When the Inspirations showed up, we knew there was gonna be some serious singing. Unfortunately, over the years Cissy and I didn't get to know each other out of the studio. But I have always regarded her as a friend, although I feel she is confused these days about certain things regarding my family and statements that she and Gladys Knight have both made about me. (I realize that Gladys has been under an extreme amount of pressure having to do with career disappointments. I truly am sympathetic and will pray for her.)

This was the period when Carolyn broke out with some serious writing. I recorded her "Ain't Nobody (Gonna Turn Me Around)" and "Ain't No Way." As the years went on, I continued recording Carolyn's compositions, which eventually earned her a beautiful living. She was doing what she loved best and making money at it. I was pleased to help my family. And I was glad that Erma's "Piece of My Heart" was a hit. The song was covered by Janis Joplin, but Erma's version was stronger.

As soon as I earned money, I was quick to help my family. (A jealous someone from New Bethel had dropped a dime on my father, telling the IRS that he was earning billions. That was a wild exaggeration, but from that day on, the IRS never lightened up on Daddy.) And speaking of money, I wasn't doing too bad. I was proud of the money I was making. I had worked long and hard to get to this point, and I was intent on enjoying it.

I tithed and gave to many charities, including Jesse Jackson's Operation Breadbasket, the NAACP, Operation PUSH, UNICEF, and Easter Seals, and I lent my appearance many times to the muscular dystrophy cause. I was in a position I had never before been in: I could express myself in so many ways. I was truly blessed.

# Queen for All Seasons

It was in the sixties that a noted disc jockey, Pervis Spann, anointed me Queen of Soul in the city of Chicago on the stage of the Regal Theater. He placed a beautifully bejeweled crown on my head, and I still cherish the memory of my silver-sequined gown. The only queens I had known of were Dinah Washington and Elizabeth I and II. To be considered worthy of the same title held by Dinah was an honor of the highest order.

In February 1968, Mayor James Cavanaugh declared Aretha Franklin Day after I performed in Detroit's Cobo Hall. That was a performance to remember. Fans stomped and screamed until I thought the rafters were coming down. I was touched and so thrilled when I learned Dr. King had flown in as a surprise guest. I introduced him. The audience of eleven thousand went wild in ovation, the brothers and sisters stomping, cheering, and whistling. Then Dr. King surprised me with a special honor, the Drum Beat Award, from the Southern Christian Leadership Conference. That was the last time I saw the great man alive.

My personal memories of Dr. King's loving-kindness and profound humanity are precious. I also loved his wit; as a storyteller, he could captivate for hours.

I flew to his funeral in Atlanta from Detroit. The flights were all booked, so I chartered a plane. Also unable to get seats on a commercial airline, Gladys Knight and the Pips called and asked if they might come along. I was delighted to accommodate them. It was a sad trip, all of us with our own private thoughts but still trying to keep our spirits up. They played games in the back, and I sat quietly in front and read. When we arrived in Atlanta and deplaned, I was surprised that neither Gladys nor the Pips bothered to say thank you for the free ride. It hardly mattered, though. My thoughts were on Dr. King.

During the procession, I walked in the street somewhere behind the King family. Afterward, I visited with Coretta King, who was in bed, to convey my sympathies. I recall seeing Eartha Kitt and Leontyne Price. Miss Price and I sat across from each other on one of the shuttles after the service, but neither of us spoke. I paid my respects and left the city, knowing that, given Dr. King's shining example, our world was surely a better place. But I wondered if decades, perhaps centuries, might pass before we would see another man like him.

The mourning for Dr. King was not an easy process for any of us. When I hear his voice or see his many appearances on TV—or the voice and likeness of my father—I'm reminded of those great men whose words and deeds really meant something. They had so much integrity, and their word was *really* their bond. They were leaders of a generation of giants whom I was so privileged to know and for whom I sang—and still sing—the songs of Zion. That generation provided us with an example of not only religious conviction but high political consciousness. I see some men of that caliber today and love them for everything they represent. They press on toward the mark of a higher calling, and, in spite of great odds, they excel.

I'm talking about men like John Hope Franklin, Dr. Benjamin Mays of Morehouse College, Benjamin Hooks, Quincy Jones, Andrew Young, Dr. Claude Young, Mayor Dennis Archer of Detroit, Reverend Jesse Jackson, and so many others. As they say at Morehouse, when the bell rings, these men answer.

In the midst of so many cataclysmic events, my career continued to surge. I was living out of a suitcase, running from the studio to concerts, on and off planes every day. I'd be in New York for breakfast, Atlanta for lunch, and Los Angeles for dinner. Don't tell me I wasn't flying.

The hits kept coming. My third Atlantic album, *Lady Soul,* was filled with big singles. "Chain of Fools," Don Covay's gritty anthem about love obsession, shot to the top of the charts. I came up with the idea for the guitarist Cornell Dupree to try a Pops Staples muddy-Mississippi guitar twang, helping to give "Chain" a minor, funky flavor.

Jerry Wexler came up with the title, and Carole King and Gerry Goffin wrote the song "(You Make Me Feel Like) A Natural Woman," which proved a natural for me. I'm still singing and loving it. My sister Carolyn came up with another winner, "Ain't No Way." As I listened to the lyrics, I realized there was something on Carolyn's mind that I was unaware of; I knew we needed to talk. I can't say enough about the beauty and depth of my sister's ballads.

I wrote "Since You've Been Gone (Sweet Sweet Baby)," which had a great groove. Between the covers—Ray Charles's "Come Back Baby," the Young Rascals' "Groovin'," Curtis Mayfield's "People Get Ready," and James Brown's "Money Won't Change You"—*Lady Soul* became an instant classic. In addition to the guys from Muscle Shoals, Jerry Wexler brought in soul man extraordinaire Bobby Womack and notable English guitarist Eric Clapton.

Speaking of Womack, I remember one night after the Coconut Grove in Los Angeles when we cruised down to Tommy's Burgers and turned the radio all the way up while Bobby killed "That's the Way I Feel About Cha." I loved it. That song and his music changed my impression of him altogether.

My next album, *Aretha Now,* included two other smashes: "I Say a Little Prayer," a cover of Dionne Warwick's hit that became a hit of my own, and "I Can't See Myself Leaving You," another Ronnie Shannon special. He was an earthy writer and a good guy.

Four big albums in less than two years, and now I was going on tour to France, Holland, Switzerland, Germany, and England in the spring of 1968. I recorded *Aretha in Paris* at the Olympia Theatre. I had been especially looking forward to the City of Lights. I do love Paris, from the sidewalk cafés and the lovers embracing in public to the chic fashion of people on the streets, the Eiffel Tower, the Champs-Élysées, and the Arc de Triomphe. I also love the Hotel George V, with its plush bedding and pillows that you could sink into and fall fast asleep on after a concert or evening of romance, or a day spent shopping the city's glamorous stores.

I love most things French—the culture, the cuisine, and the romantic intonation of the language. While performing at the Olympia, though, I noticed the audience was especially quiet; I had never performed for such a quiet audience. I was concerned about whether they were enjoying the concert, being used to very emotional audiences, but when it was over I learned that the French don't respond until they have heard it all. They are very careful listeners. The standing ovation went on for the longest; I was glowing inside. The discriminating French turned out to be among my biggest fans.

Carolyn, Wyline Ivy, and Charnessa Jones were my background singers on that trip, and immediately after the concert we hit the streets, pounding the pavement up and down the Champs-Élysées and buying everything in sight, crisscrossing the major boulevards and tipping in and out of every upscale store in sight. Paris exceeded my expectations.

On a foggy day in London town, we had the good fortune to be met by Ahmet Ertegun, president of Atlantic Records and husband of Mica Ertegun, interior decorator extraordinaire, the most chichi of New York decorators. Ahmet took us to Carnaby Street and the most quaint boutiques. I admired the golden Rolls-Royce in which he was being chauffeured but found it a little uncomfortable to be riding so high; the seats were more elevated than I was accustomed to.

Even though it was Jerry Wexler, not Ahmet, who supervised the bulk of my Atlantic work, I would sometimes visit Ahmet after the sessions. I found him fascinating. The son of a Turkish ambassador, he combined a refined sense of European elegance and style with genuine love and knowledge of African American culture. He was so real. After all, Ahmet was the man who began Atlantic and signed artists like Ruth Brown, Big Joe Turner, and Clyde McPhatter. Ahmet and his brother Nesuhi were astute and savvy record men with great savoir faire and distinct urbanity. Ahmet was also a songwriter of merit. (A couple of years later I covered his "Don't Play That Song," originally a big hit for Ben E. King, on my *Spirit in the Dark* album.) As time went on, I grew more enchanted with Europe. We stopped next in Switzerland, where I performed for a young prince and princess. Everyone in the club that evening was buzzing about the royalty in the front row.

I felt very special winging home to Detroit and going through customs. The direction of my career was still straight up. I was asked to sing the national anthem at the Democratic convention in 1968, the same tumultuous Chicago convention that nominated Hubert Humphrey. As I readied myself in the small, dark dressing room with just a curtain, chair, and mirror, I had no idea pandemonium had erupted outside, centering on the protesters against the Vietnam War. Before those stormy events of August, though, the summer started off on another difficult note.

When I learned I was going to be put on the cover of *Time* magazine, I was excited and pleased. They were calling the story "The Sound of Soul" and saw me as a symbol of the soul explosion that had enthralled the nation. As it turned out, though, *Time* became the main source of the false and thoughtless lies about my mother abandoning her children, which Gladys Knight and Cissy Houston perpetuated in their memoirs. I don't understand why neither lady bothered to ask me whether the story was true before printing it, since, like all public figures, they themselves must have been the subjects of incorrect press as well.

The article also painted me as a woman trapped by the blues, like Bessie Smith or Billie Holiday. Nothing could be further from the truth. I am Aretha, upbeat, straight-ahead, and not to be worn out by men and left singing the blues. *Time* described alleged incidents between Ted White and myself, some of which were not reported accurately. Even worse, my own words were taken out of context and turned around to make the writer's point. Due to the stature of *Time,* the mistakes were picked up by countless writers in the years ahead and reported as fact. For a long time I declined many interviews because I did not trust certain journalists. I didn't want my words taken out of context; I certainly didn't want a false picture painted of myself. In my professional growth and maturity, however, I have learned how to address such matters and have done many wonderful (and accurately reported) interviews.

One correct point in the article was that my relationship with White was beyond repair. We agreed to divorce. Arrangements were made for me to fly down from Miami to Haiti. It was over within a matter of minutes; no one was present other than me, a gentleman I refer to as my alter ego, and the judge. The details were simple—he kept the boat, I got our home on Sorrento in Detroit, and the copyrights on my songs were split down the middle.

I began a relationship with a man I will refer to only as Mr. Mystique. Because he is a public figure, I prefer to protect his privacy. I do not wish to embarrass him or break our code of secrecy. I cannot exclude him from my book, however, because of my love for him and because for many years he was an on-again, off-again part of my romantic life. Our friendship never became known to anyone other than ourselves. We discovered each other in Atlanta. I was too naïve and bloody in love with him to realize the ultimate bottom line. Our priorities and goals were totally different. For me, it was love with all of my heart.

Our rapport was magical. Conversation came easy. He was a man of endless charm and wit. I always felt we were a natural, a dream couple. We talked intimately and sensitively well into the midnight hour. We were friends. And then we became lovers.

It happened in New York on a sweltering summer evening that extended well into the A.M. He was flying out that night but missed the flight, so we checked into a motel. Early in the morning, looking at him sleeping so comfortably and beautifully, I wrote on the mirror with my lipstick before I tiptoed out of the room, "I love you, baby." My heart and soul were filled to the brim. I wiped away the words, though, when I realized I might be recognized by the maids. But we lost sight of each other, and in the early sixties I met a group of dazzling entertainers.

The Temptations were sensational singers and showmen, and a

few of them had reputations in the field of romance. I had met them all, beginning with Paul Williams, who had a friend only a few doors from my dad on LaSalle. I loved their music, and I especially enjoyed David Ruffin and Dennis Edwards, two of the great soul singers of our time.

In 1968 David quit to go on his own, and Dennis Edwards took his place. Dennis and I shared some of the most surprising and memorable moments a couple could have. I must note here that Erma hadn't met Dennis or the Temptations yet. I had a house in Detroit on Sorrento just off Outer Drive. One day the doorbell rang. (In Detroit people will often drop by without calling.) When I opened the door, the Temptations were standing on the front porch.

I invited them in, and they explained that they had music they wanted me to hear, songs they wanted me to perform with them. One Temptation was tempting me a lot more than the others. My attention kept drifting from the songs to this beautiful six-foot man in the white silk suit. I mean, he was *wearing* that suit. The Temps were singing, but I really didn't digest or hear anything. Dennis and I made eye contact and drifted off to my den, where we sat on a leather couch verbally familiarizing ourselves with each other. As one thing led to another, we embraced. I was definitely on cloud nine. It was so natural and spontaneous, and he could sing his you-know-what off. It was all just too good to be true. Where had he been all of my life?

Dennis had a fiery, gospel-trained voice and vocally stood second to none. His rep as a singer was rivaled only by his rep as a ladies' man. My brother Cecil tried to pull my hemline about Dennis early on. But I was willing to play anyway. Some lessons take longer than others.

Meanwhile, my sister Erma and I had a serious misunderstanding over Mr. Edwards. Perhaps a better word is fight. We were at my dad's when out of the blue she threw a glass at me. As I saw the glass whiz past my head, I said to myself, *I know she didn't just throw this glass at me.* Well, the fight was on.

I honestly never felt there had been a real relationship between Erma and Dennis, and still don't. Erma was and is my sister, and I know when she's really serious about someone. She was never seriously interested in Dennis. Erma was in and out of love every other week. Besides, I would never intentionally or knowingly become involved with anyone that I felt Erma or anyone in my family was interested in. Our relationship as sisters is far more valuable to me. Anyway, Daddy had us take the fight upstairs. He wanted us to get it out of our systems before breaking it up at the optimum moment.

Many of my encounters with Dennis were wonderful, others weren't. For a long time he kept an apartment at 1300 Lafayette in downtown Detroit. It was one of the first high-rises overlooking the Detroit River. One time I flew out to Detroit to visit him unannounced, and a young lady answered the door. She invited me in, and after waiting so long for Dennis to return, I got tired and decided to lie across the bed and take a nap. When I awoke Dennis still had not come home. The woman and I were chatting when I decided to call a few friends and have a party right there at Dennis's place. So I called Charles Cook, among a number of other people, and we were well into the party and in high gear, boogying all over the house. When he showed up, to put it mildly, Dennis wasn't thrilled with the party in progress and cleared everyone out like a Texas roundup.

I realized I had been far too presumptuous—I was definitely wrong to invite people to his home without his approval. Needless to say, it was not one of our better evenings. However, the next day when I put the pot on in the kitchen—hot-water corn bread, greens, and so on—he eased in and began kissing me on the back of the neck. He certainly knows where to put it when he wants a favorable response. Was it live or was it Memorex? Aretha or the greens?

Dennis and I had a strong physical attraction for each other. As artists, we admired each other as well. But that was it. It took me awhile, but eventually I got the T (the Truth) about Mr. D.

Meanwhile, another man entered my life. Thank God.

# And Along Came Wolf

In spite of a couple of unmentionables, I will always love and appreciate Ken Cunningham for being the man that he was— genuine, unfull of shit, compassionate, and giving. I thought of him as my alter ego.

I met Ken, whom I nicknamed Wolf, in Miami Beach while I was staying at the fabulous Fontainebleau, *the* hotel in those days. He arranged a meeting to discuss the possibility of my investing in his company, the New Breeders, a group of young and attractive independent black businessmen who had set up an impressive system of clothing and shoe manufacturing. They were designers as well as manufacturers, specializing in African-styled garbs, exotic fabrics, gorgeous dashikis, sandals, and dress shoes. Their factory was in the Bronx, and Wolf had an interest in it. He was a New Breeder.

Slim, bronze, and strikingly handsome, Wolf came in wearing a gray pin-striped dashiki suit that spoke well for the company he represented. He had a beautiful, big freedom 'fro. He was also lighthearted and funny. This was a time when black entrepreneurs were on the rise. Daddy had been preaching black pride for decades, and we as a people had rediscovered how beautiful black truly was and were echoing, "Say it loud, I'm black and I'm proud." Wolf and I embodied that pride. He recognized and met my needs in a way that no one else ever had, and he saw what no one else did. You could call it love at first sight. Much to my delight, he decided to stay. His trip to Miami was extended, and the New Breeders' loss was my gain.

When we met, Wolf was separated and in the process of getting a divorce. I did not feel I was breaking up anyone's relationship; as I heard it, the relationship was already over. He had a beautiful little girl named Paige, a miniature version of Wolf, who came to live with us. Right off the top, Paige stole my heart. She was like the little girl I never had, bright and sweet and sensitive. Today she could easily sit down any high-fashion model.

Back in New York, I found myself with a man who seemed to care more about me—and what was good for me—than any man who had preceded him. He appreciated me as a woman and helped me to more fully appreciate the natural aspects of myself. I blossomed under his strong support. We were young adults reaching and striving to be mature and responsible parents. A line in the song "April Fools" expressed our struggle well: "Are we just April fools? I don't care, true love has found us now."

Wolf even helped me change my approach to makeup. I stopped shaving my eyebrows and using pencils and went back to a natural look with a much lighter touch. I lost weight and wore my hair in an Afro; I began to appreciate myself as a beautiful black woman. Wolf was also interested in African poetry, art, and sculpture. He loved jazz and music of all kinds. And he had friends who, like Wolf, were intellectual and positive people. His friends—brothers like Jimmy Dunn, Ellis Fleming, Howard Davis, Chuck Brown of NBC Washington, and Pat and Roy McCurdy—became my friends. They became part of our social life, now filled with exciting discussions, not to mention downright fun.

I brought my three sons to the relationship. Together, Wolf and I had a son of our own, Kecalf. (Kecalf stands for "Ken E. Cunningham/Aretha Louise Franklin," and we pronounce it "Kelf.") Kecalf was a beautiful blessing and ongoing joy in my life. The day that he was born, Carolyn went to the hospital with me, and Wolf met us there with balloons and a giant, all-year sucker; our son was delivered by our friend and family doctor, Dr. Claude Young. I thank God for all my children.

Wolf and I moved to New York and set up housekeeping in an exclusive high-rise on Fifty-third Street and Seventh Avenue. Ed McMahon of *The Tonight Show* was one of our closest neighbors. We had a luxurious penthouse on the thirtieth floor, with two levels joined by a circular staircase. There were three bedrooms, two baths, plush orange carpeting, mirrored closets, and a wet bar. I kept an electric piano at the window facing a spectacular view of the city. Kecalf lived with us. Clarence and Eddie were back in Detroit, cared for by Big Mama, while Teddy lived with his paternal grandmother and his dad. For a long while my domestic life had stability and balance.

When I was gone, Big Mama took the boys to church regularly and sat right at the foot of the pulpit, ringing out, "Yes, Lord" or "You're mighty right," when my dad or others were preaching. She had a significant hand in laying the foundation of my sons' lives rooted in church and the gospel. I couldn't always be with my children, but I was there as much as possible, always communicating with them regularly. In my absence, Big Mama was a positive influence. When I began to establish myself, the boys came to live with me. After discussing it with Wolf, I enrolled them in private school.

In 1969 Jerry Wexler and I decided to change up the formula by putting me in front of a jazz big band. That album became *Soul '69* and had me singing an assortment, everything from revisiting "Today I Sing the Blues" (the first thing I did on Columbia, nine years earlier) to "Tracks of My Tears," one of Smokey Robinson's more fabulous compositions.

Jerry was surprised when I wanted to sing "Gentle on My Mind," which had been a huge hit for Glen Campbell. But I have always appreciated all kinds of music, country included. I love the uniqueness of the lyrics. The veteran trumpeter Joe Newman solos on this song, just as Ray Charles's sax man Fathead Newman solos on most of the other selections. Proud to say, the album has become a classic, like almost all of my Atlantic material.

If I was making a strong musical statement in this accelerated period of my career, I was also making a strong fashion statement. I think the Supremes and Diana Ross would agree with me. I say that because I was wearing stage clothing designed by a gentleman from Detroit named Otis Caver. He had designed some wonderful oversized hats for me. I also wore some highly decorative Art Deco beaded gowns by Boyd Clopton of Los Angeles, one of which I wore on *The Tonight Show* and also to the Oscars. Shortly thereafter, I noted that Diana and the Supremes came out with almost the same outfit—oversized hats and Art Deco beaded gowns—and were sporting it on the first Motown special. We did have good taste, didn't we, girls?

Speaking of the Oscars, I will always remember the moment I was introduced by Frank Sinatra and sang "Funny Girl." Afterward I went to the Governor's Ball, where, for the first time, I saw an entire ceiling of a grand ballroom covered with fresh yellow roses. It was at the Beverly Hilton, where Diahann Carroll, beautifully gowned by Arnold Scaasi, made a late entrance and drew a small crowd in the center of the room. Everything, from the soft glow of the tapered candles to the exquisite crystal and china, was perfection itself.

Outside the world of show business, the real world was in the throes of change. Events were moving with alarming speed. In 1968, after Dr. King's assassination, riots broke out all over. Detroit was in flames, and it would take the city decades to recover. When I came home from New York, I was shocked and saddened to see the bullet-riddled house a few doors from my dad's, the National Guard still set up at Central High School with tanks and guns. Sections of the city were burned to cinders. Other cities were suffering the same agony. That year Richard Nixon beat Hubert Humphrey for the presidency. The Vietnam War was still going on, and I would receive an occasional letter from Vaughn, stationed over there. Concurrently the Apollo space missions were going full blast; soon men would be walking on the moon. (Big Mama, by the way, never believed they went to the moon. She thought they were somewhere on a movie set. Big Mama cracked me up.)

As the sixties became the seventies, soul music was still leading the field, perhaps because it expressed the raw emotion people were feeling. On my first album released in 1970, *This Girl's in Love with You,* I sang two Beatles songs, "Let It Be" and "Eleanor Rigby." Jerry Wexler has written that Paul McCartney and John Lennon wrote "Let It Be" expressly for me, but that was not true. The minute I heard the song, though, I loved it. Ditto for "Eleanor Rigby." Early on I recognized the Beatles' charm as showmen and their talent as writers.

The song "Share Your Love with Me" was something I heard Bobby "Blue" Bland sing. Loved the melody. Bluc is the consummate bluesman. To keep things current, Jerry suggested I sing "The Weight," a song by the Band, a superhot group at the time who had been Bob Dylan's backup band. I liked the song, but to this day don't have the foggiest notion of what the hook was about.

Certainly I understood "Call Me." That's because I wrote it, based on a treasured memory of a beautiful spring day in New York City, one of those rare Manhattan afternoons when the air is fresh, the sun bright, the sky a cloudless blue. Two lovers, hand in hand, walk down Park Avenue. They must part. As they walk away from each other, they turn back for one last glance. The man says, "I love you"; the woman replies, "I love you too." They linger for a few seconds, not wanting the moment to end. Finally the woman says, "Call me . . . call me the moment you get there . . . the hour . . . the minute . . . the second . . . call me, baby." It was the story of me and Wolf.

In the course of my relationship with Wolf, our love was tested. My friendship with Dennis Edwards had not entirely run its course. On one occasion when the Temps were at their peak, playing the Copa, Dennis had his valet call to invite me to the Sheraton. I accepted the invitation and stopped by his room. I have a vivid memory of Dennis standing in the bathroom, shaving, shirtless, so sexxxxxxy and just plain beautiful. He made several interesting comments and overtures that were more than appreciated. Complicating matters more, Mr. Mystique was in town and asked me to accompany him to the Copa to see the Temps. I passed. In fact, out of consideration and respect for Wolf, I decided to pass on both Dennis and Mr. Mystique. Not long after this, Wolf found a ring Dennis had given me, a platinum setting with a single, sizable, white, white diamond. It was Dennis's ring. I wanted it, and he wanted me to have it. However, I sent it back to him, insured for five thousand dollars, and enclosed a note. I thought that would be the end of it. Wolf was obviously a loyal man who had my best interests at heart, as I had his. But my heart was still not entirely free of temptations.

The Temps were playing at the Performing Arts Center in Saratoga Springs, New York, and Dennis asked me to fly up. I considered going. Wolf was cool and confident enough in himself and in our relationship to say, "Hey, I want you to find out how you really feel and make a decision." Wolf was that kind of guy—secure enough to give me the freedom to find out for myself how I really felt. Anyhow, I found myself on a night flight to upstate New York. I took a cab to the hotel, arrived before the Temps, and checked in. I left a message at the desk for Dennis, who called upon his arrival. Just before walking onstage, he gave me his money pouch to hold. I was impressed by his trust in me. The Temps were monstrous as usual. Standing in the wings watching Dennis—admiring another singer that I was involved with—was new and different for me. I was as thrilled as any of the screaming fans reaching for them at the foot of the stage, and I loved to see Dennis do his thing. Next morning, I thought we'd fly back to New York together. "Why don't we ride in the limo instead?" Dennis suggested. "That'll give us hours of privacy."

It turned out to be one of the great limo rides in the history of limos. We joked and laughed and shared many moments of fun all the way back to New York. When we reached the city at evening time, the weather was warm, bewitching. The world was at peace. It had been a beautiful trip; I was on cloud nine, and it wasn't just my imagination. Out of that experience I wrote a song that I'd record a little later called "Day Dreaming."

"Day dreaming and I'm thinking of you," I sang. "He's the kind of guy that would say, 'Hey, baby, let's get away, let's go someplace, where I don't care' . . . He's the kind of guy that you give your everything, your trust, your heart, all of your love till death do you part . . . I want to be what he wants when he wants it and whenever he needs it . . . And when he's lonesome and feeling love-starved, I'll be there to feed it."

The lyrics I wrote were straight from the heart but naïve, though I didn't realize it then. We were two entirely different people with two different sets of principles. It was destined to come undone. It was just a matter of time. My naïveté came to a screeching halt when I went to visit Dennis in California. I now know what Wolf meant when he said, "When you know who you are, you will know who I am."

That California trip came after a difficult concert in Cherry Hill, New Jersey. I'd been told a promoter was threatening my life. It has been so long ago now that I don't really recall why Cecil said he was so upset. I believe his promotion was poor and he didn't have the money to pay me. But I performed with more than adequate security and left immediately after the concert, excited about the prospect of being with Dennis.

The Temps were appearing on *The Sonny and Cher Comedy Hour,* the hottest thing going at the time. Dennis was to meet me at the airport, but he never showed. Bad sign. I took a limo to his hotel, where I was told he was out. I asked for the key, saying that I was Mrs. Edwards. The man finally showed up after several hours, saying the Sonny and Cher show was responsible for his delay. By then my patience had run out; I had already booked a flight back East. Dennis was sensitive and apologetic, though, and talked me into staying the night. The next day the Temps were off to Japan. But I later learned that Dennis was not being straight up with me. I was beginning to get the T from credible sources concerning other ladies as well. But more on Mr. Edwards's intrigues a little later.

Cecil was the most important member of my professional team.

During the early part of my career, he had served as assistant pastor in Daddy's church. Like my father, he was a gifted orator and serious student of the Bible. Cecil could speak eloquently and preach. During the days when I was without management, Daddy had Cecil come on the road to help me out. I recall one meeting with our accountants and lawyers when a slew of numbers were being bantered about. Everyone was trying to project concert grosses. Suddenly Cecil stood up and said, "Here's the number you've been looking for," without a calculator or pen. Before anyone else in the room and within moments, Cecil had figured it out. I was deeply impressed and, from then on, had absolute trust in my brother and his business acumen.

Meanwhile, my love for Wolf deepened. He helped me enter a period of strong and steady growth, both as woman and as musician. Wolf called it the Age of Aretha. I loved that phrase, by which he meant people were growing up to my music, getting married, having babies, defining their youth and making memories that would last a lifetime. I loved being part of all those memories.

# Sizzling in the Seventies

W e loved to cook. And, believe me, Wolf could throw down in the kitchen. Everyone in Wolf's family could cook, and we spent lots of time creating culinary masterpieces while listening to WBLS's premier deejay Frankie Crocker's early evening mellow rap.

The changes in the culture continued to influence our world. Protest was in the air. In 1971 the Supreme Court reversed Muhammad Ali's draft-refusal conviction. A lifelong Ali fan, I was there for many of his illustrious fights, including his mammoth battles with Joe Frazier. I would be out of my seat and standing on it, screaming with the rest of his fans. And later all that screaming cost me and Wolf a small fortune. Here's the story:

I had spared no expense in buying Wolf a beautiful watch from Van Cleef & Arpels for his birthday, a fabulous timepiece. That night we went to the Waldorf to watch the Ali-Foreman fight, the famous rope-a-dope encounter from Zaire, on closed circuit. Well, Wolf was so excited, jumping up and down and flailing his arms around, he didn't even know the watch had either flown off his wrist or been snatched off. We were out on Park Avenue before we realized what had happened. We hurried back to the hotel, but the cleaning crew had already vacuumed, and there wasn't a trace of Van Cleef & Arpels. Ali had won, but we'd lost.

Another cultural phenomenon of the times was the flower children. Hippies were everywhere. I liked their colorful garb and their love-the-world philosophy. Who could be against peace? They were gentle kids, and many of them were whites expressing a genuine love for black music. As far as my own music, I wasn't sure how hippies reacted to me until I found myself booked at Bill Graham's Fillmore West in San Francisco, the Taj Mahal of flower power.

Fortunately, Atlantic taped the concert, and the record, *Aretha Live at Fillmore West,* is still available. It was a night to remember. Whatever the capacity of the hall, three times that number were there. They stood toe to toe, wall to wall. The place was so packed it might have been scary were it not for the warm and accepting vibe. The flower children embraced me with gusto. Instead of my usual touring band, led by Donald Townes, I used the great King Curtis and the Kingpins, a soul band supreme. Billy Preston, a James Cleveland protégé, was on organ. The rhythm section— Cornell Dupree, Jerry Jemmott, Bernard Purdie, and Pancho Morales—was burning, while the Sweethearts of Soul—my cousin Brenda, Margaret Branch, and Pat Smith—honed the background harmonies. I selected certain songs—"Love the One You're With," "Bridge over Troubled Water," "Eleanor Rigby," "Make It with You"—with special appeal to this audience, but it was the soul classics that lit up the night and stole thunder from the heavens.

Ruthie Bowen, one of my agents, had seen Ray Charles a week earlier and told him about the Fillmore gig. That night, when I heard he was there, I couldn't resist the idea of a duet. But I knew Ray, and I knew the only way he'd come up was if I went and personally brought him to the stage. So I did, reappearing before the ecstatic crowd with the Genius himself. Echoing Flip Wilson's famous line, I said, "I discovered Ray Charles!" We sang "Spirit in the Dark." Ray didn't know all the lyrics, but that made it better. The Right Reverend made up his own, and, between the two of us, soul oozed out of every pore of the Fillmore. All the planets were aligned right that night, because when the music came down, it was as real and righteous as any recording I'd ever made.

On my most recent record I'd done a studio version of "Spirit in the Dark"—the title of the album—but the version with Ray was something special. On the *Spirit* album I sang two songs associated with B. B. King—"The Thrill Is Gone" and "Why I Sing the Blues." When I was a kid, I'd skated to Dinah Washington's "That's All I Want from You" at the Arcadia. I loved that song. When I sang it on *Spirit,* my mind went back to those couples-only songs when Romeo of the rink and I would back-skate all hugged up.

*Spirit in the Dark* also included another gem from Carolyn, "Pullin'." Carolyn kept pulling down those hit songs. "Try Matty's" was something I wrote about a hot soul-food hangout on Dexter in northwest Detroit. Some of the best ribs you've ever wrapped your lips around. And "Oh No Not My Baby" was a song associated with Maxine Brown, a formidable vocalist who'd married a cousin of ours and had modest success in the early sixties.

⌒

I established a nice break in my recording routine by going down to Florida yearly. Jerry Wexler set up Criteria Studios in Miami, the scene of some of our best sessions. It was especially wonderful to go south in the winter. When Detroit and New York were in deep freeze, Wolf and I would be lounging around the pool of the Fontainebleau in bikinis and tank tops. The studio vibe couldn't have been more relaxed. The team—Ree, Jerry, Tom Dowd, and Arif Mardin—was getting stronger. These were the days when, thanks to Wexler, I also met Donny Hathaway, an introverted musical genius, a friendly person with a deep music personality. And it was with Donny on organ that I created one of my greatest hits, "Rock Steady."

The rhythm section was mean—Cornell Dupree on guitar, Chuck Rainey on bass, Bernard Purdie on drums, and me on piano. But it was Donny who added that high organ line that gives "Rock Steady" such extra added flow. I love that organ line. Like Ray Charles and me, Donny came out of the sanctified church as a singer and pianist. His grandmother was a minister, and he had gospel written all over him. Also like Ray and me, he was multi-musical the way some folks are multilingual. With his rich voice and unique style, Donny had his own signature. He was a young master and a soul artist of tremendous talent, easy and quiet.

Wolf and I also saw Donny many years later in Nashville, where he played us some new things, which, to my ears, sounded a little far-out. Soon after that he was gone, dead at the tragically young age of thirty-three. Despite his youth, he left behind a beautiful body of work and influenced schools of soul singers. I didn't have the personal relationship with Donny that Roberta Flack, his duet partner, enjoyed. But I admired him greatly. Historians should not forget him. And scholars should get it right: Donny Hathaway was one of the great communicators and masters of soul.

Donny played on six of the songs included on my album *Young, Gifted and Black,* including my version of "I've Been Loving You Too Long," Otis Redding's riveting ballad. Otis also died decades before his time, another major star in the great galaxy of soul. *Young, Gifted and Black* may have been my most personal—and most romantic—album to date. "April Fools," the Burt Bacharach–Hal David song, hit home. I thought of Wolf and myself, a couple of young people in love. The line "I don't care . . . true love has found us now" mirrored my feelings about a relationship that was deepening each day to the point where I was a little concerned. After all, I had never been involved at this level of maturity and seriousness. But Wolf was doing wonders, encouraging me to be myself, and I was feeling especially creative. In addition to "Day Dreaming," "Rock Steady," and "All the King's Horses"—a sad song about the end of an affair—I wrote "First Snow in Kokomo," a poem of mine set to music. I was feeling free and willing to take creative chances.

I wrote "Kokomo" in Kokomo; the story was set in Wolf's mother's Indiana home during the chill of winter. In free-verse style, I painted a picture of a blissful January afternoon when we pulled into the small, peaceful midwestern town to visit his family. It was me, Wolf, and all the intellectual New Breeders, guys into photography and art and music and manufacturing. We were just hanging out. Wolf was learning to blow his horn and wearing us out with it—he loved to noodle on trumpet—while his pal Jimmy Dunn was playing bass. Little details of daily life. Another friend, Reggie, and his wife were expecting a baby. By the end of the song, which I arranged out of rhythm—there's no steady beat but instead the irregular rhythm of real life—the baby, called Moishe, Jimmy and Jerrie Dunn's son, is born.

If "First Snow in Kokomo" sounds kicked-back, it's because I was kicked-back. I became very close to and part of Wolf's family. I was close to his mom, Mrs. Virginia Brent (God rest her soul), and enjoyed her company in addition to the intellectual conversation with Wolf's family. She was so down-to-earth and had a wonderfully dry, very sharp wit, and we had many a good conversation.

Walking through the Fontainebleau hallway with a bag full of pigs' feet and bones, Wolf and I found ourselves laughing over this incident: We had a major meal cooking on the stovetop in our suite, and one evening after dinner, on my way to the incinerator, the bag, wet at the bottom, burst open. Pigs' feet bones flew everywhere, rolling down those luxurious hallways. The Fontainebleau hotel had been officially christened by me.

From Miami, Wolf and I took a number of romantic trips to the Caribbean and beyond. Once we sailed to the Bahamas, cooking all the way—Wolf's dad; daughter, Paige; and my cousin Brenda and her husband, James. We also vacationed in Barbados, where we shot the cover of my first gospel album for Atlantic, *Amazing Grace,* at Sam Lord's castle, a real castle turned hotel. And it was in Barbados where we ran into Nina Simone, whose song "Young, Gifted and Black" was the title of my current album. We had several refreshing poolside lunches with Nina. She was with her daughter Lisa and still upset about the political upheaval in America. I liked Nina. She was a proud, outspoken, and earthy independent artist who, like Marvin Gaye, could incorporate strong social commentary into her music.

In Bermuda we went a little overboard riding bikes. Too many falls on our butts, too much road rash. I had my birthday party in an old cave with Wolf, Bernard Purdie, Chuck Rainey, Erma Dupree, and the gang. By the way, it was in Bermuda where I heard the group talking about a new young vocalist by the name of Natalie Cole who was appearing in town. I had already read her story in *Ebony* magazine and was very surprised and flattered when she intimated that she had been strongly influenced by me. Carolyn and the rest of the group went in to catch her show. Wolf and I crashed. Natalie is another story I'll get to a little later.

Our jaunts to exotic islands were wonderful as I discovered the world along with my own independence. After so many years of being sheltered by my dad and the couple of dominating-type men I dated, Wolf was a godsend, a welcome change and more right for me. Still, there were moments of unease. I remember, for example, being somewhat frightened in Caracas. I felt a hell of a long way away from home. Wolf and I were sunning out on the balcony when a certain apprehension came over me. Then the group Chicago came on the radio and immediately soothed my soul. The lead singer was trying to sound like Smokey, and I found his voice comforting. It was a spiritual experience, helping me realize I had nothing to fear.

In London we stayed at the ultraswanky Savoy. We flew in two of my sons, Clarence and Eddie, who were in the adjoining room. All of a sudden I heard commotion, things being knocked over. I opened the adjoining door to find the boys going at it toe-to-toe. Wolf broke them up. Parenting can be trying.

In Viareggio I had a wonderful time, mainly because of the beautiful butter-soft leather goods and great weather. We bought leather pants at twenty-five dollars a pair. I can't tell you how many pairs I bought. I cleaned out the store. We arrived at our hotel in Antibes in the south of France just at the start of a jazz festival. It was a soft summer night, and we took in the sounds of Lionel Hampton and Rahssaan Roland Kirk floating on the night air. You could hear them throughout the hotel as the elevator whisked us up to our suite. We also traveled to the French Riviera, accompanied by my booking agent, Ruthie Bowen. She and I went shopping and sight-seeing up and down the promenade at Cannes in spiked heels and bikinis, truly letting it all hang out. The wolf whistles (and the wolves) were right behind us. You must remember at the time I was a sexy size ten or twelve, and, well, when in Rome, do as the Romans. Cannes was absolutely agreeing with me. We also sent pictures to *Jet* magazine as proof of the dynamite time we were having in Europe. I recall one of them standing by my proud catch of an eighteen-inch fish. (Does that sound like a fish tale?)

Spain was a proud moment. Forty thousand fans crowded into a bullfight arena, throwing flowers at the stage and throwing each other up and down. I saw it there long before it began here. After their wildly enthusiastic response to my concert, there was no doubt that the Spaniards had soul.

# City of Dreams

⌒

In the late sixties and the seventies, New York was where many of my dreams came true. I had a good man and a good career. For my Atlantic work alone I would eventually receive ten Grammys, the most, they told me, a woman had ever won. I more than appreciated the recognition from my peers. Perhaps my most memorable Grammy moment, though, was when I appreciated another artist. It happened at the 1972 Grammy ceremonies.

I won for *Young, Gifted and Black* but gave the Grammy to Esther Phillips, who had been nominated for *From a Whisper to a Scream*. I liked Esther's record, although I didn't consider it better than mine. I gave her my Grammy because Esther was fighting personal demons, and I felt she could use encouragement. As a blues singer, she had her own thing; I wanted Esther to know that I—and the industry—supported her.

Between touring and recording, between Manhattan and Miami, I had a schedule that agreed with me. Wolf and I decided to move out of our midtown penthouse to somewhere quieter and a little more elegant. We lived at the Hotel Navarro until we found a brownstone town house on Eighty-eighth Street between Fifth and Madison, one of the most exclusive neighborhoods in New York. The tree-lined street and Upper East Side ambience gave me a sense of accomplishment; the environment was serene. We had four floors, which I furnished in a contemporary mode with touches of French and Egyptian artifacts. *Ebony* magazine did a beautiful spread on it. I had the most fabulous black potbellied stove that baked food to its ultimate best. I've always liked being domestic, and I love my home. We planted a small tree in front of our town house; it now stands fifteen feet tall.

Wolf introduced me to the delights of Cuban cuisine. We'd go over to Victor's on the West Side and order bowls of black bean soup and other spicy specialties. On some Sunday afternoons after breakfast and some gospel, I might be feeling a little lazy, so Wolf would motivate me. "Let's get going," he'd say. We'd jump on our bikes and ride down Fifth Avenue, past the Metropolitan Museum of Art and through the park.

On other days Wolf and I might cruise down to Greenwich Village, where we'd eat at little Greek or Italian food stands before sitting for a portrait by a street artist. One of my best portraits came out of the Village.

In my mind's eye, I see those days as a tremendous growth period and declaration of my independence. I was rediscovering myself. But I haven't forgotten the moments of sorrow. In 1971 my friend and bandleader King Curtis was killed by a stranger on the street. King was a key part of my music at Atlantic; he thoroughly understood soul and accompanied me, as saxist and bandleader,

My beloved mother and father.

My birthplace,
Memphis,
Tennessee.

At sweet sixteen.

Dear Aretha,
Happy Birthday!
I salute you on your natal day.
Remembering you as a talented
young lady at Alger has been among
my fondest memories. You in the
Glee Club and playing piano for the
Kindergarteners always made my day.
God gave you the talent — you developed
into the Star I knew you would be.
Love,
Mrs. Julia Mason - Preer

A birthday wish from my music teacher at Alger Elementary School, Mrs. Julia Preer.

Ms. Lola Moore, Daddy's special friend.

The one and only Sam Cooke.

Crowned Queen of Soul in the sixties by deejay Pervis Spann (the Blues Man)
in Chicago. Looking on is deejay E. Rodney Jones.

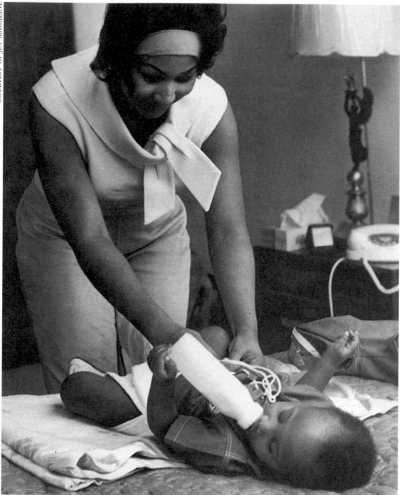

Diapering my
beautiful baby
boy Teddy.

With Jerry Wexler,
a producer who
made a difference.

Backed up by my singers in the sixties: *(from the left)* Pamela Vincent, Margaret Branch, and cousin Brenda Corbett.

At the Academy Awards ceremony in 1969, Frank Sinatra introduced me to sing the nominated song "Funny Girl."

*From the left:* Congressman John Conyers, my dad,
Jesse Jackson, and my brother Cecil.

Ken Cunningham—
the man I call my
alter ego—with
my brother Cecil
*(standing).*

Me, Ken
Cunningham,
wardrobe
mistress Larue
Manns, and my
father at the
Governors'
Ball for the
1968 Academy
Awards.

A happy bride: my formal wedding picture with Glynn.

*The Blues Brothers* brought me splendid reviews.

Recording my self-produced gospel album at the New Bethel Baptist Church
in Detroit: *(from the left)* my sister Erma, my sister Carolyn,
and my cousin Brenda.

Surrounded
by my forever
friends, Smokey
Robinson and
Sylvia Burston.

The family in
1987: *(from left)*
sisters Erma
and Carolyn,
me, and
brother Cecil
and his wife
Earline.

Thrilled to receive an honorary degree from Wayne State University in Detroit.

H. B. Barnum, my longtime musical director and friend.

Backstage with my friend and buddy Stormin' Norman Dugger.

On my way to the White House for a performance in the Rose Garden during the Clinton administration, accompanied by my longtime friends Reverend Billy Kyles and Reverend Jesse Jackson.

With the fabulous
Clive Davis, chairman
of Arista Records.

Mary J. Blige is
one of the young
artists I appreciate
and enjoy.

With Dick Alen,
my agent and
good friend.

With my good
friends, agent Ruth
Bowen *(left)* and
Larue Manns.

The 1994 Kennedy Center honorees: Kirk Douglas,
Harold Prince *(seated)*, me, Morton Gould *(seated)*, and Pete Seeger.

with exactly the right kind of funky flair. He was the man who could cook up that "Memphis Soul Stew"; his "Soul Serenade" is a permanent part of the soundtrack of my Atlantic years.

Other artistic influences had come my way in New York City. Babatunde Olatunji, the fabulous Nigerian drummer whose polyrhythms are incredible, had a school in Harlem at 125th Street and Lenox Avenue. He and I had been labelmates back in the Columbia days. Olatunji had a wonderful spirit about him, and for a while I took lessons from his dancers.

When *Vogue* magazine asked me to pose for a photo spread in the early sixties, I eagerly agreed. I've always been a reader of *Vogue, Bazaar,* and all the fashion journals. But when Wolf and I arrived for the shoot, we were amazed to find that all the models to be photographed with me were white. Wolf was upset not because there were white models but because out of so many there were no black ones, not even the token. He felt that there should have been a few brothers in the picture at least, and I agreed and did something I had never done before. I walked out. It would be another twenty years before I was asked or agreed to do *Vogue* again. However, I have enjoyed many wonderful shoots since.

At this point in my career, I would have loved to have been in a movie, but the offers that I wanted never came. However, menial and subservient parts came in and were immediately canceled out. A couple of my colleagues crossed my mind—Barbra Streisand and Diana Ross. Certainly they had no more hits than I, and I had received many awards of merit and doctorates thankfully, but Streisand had major management, and Diana had Berry Gordy. I could have used a Berry Gordy myself after Cecil. However, my faith remained firm; if it was to be, I would have movies as well; if it were not to be, so be it. I didn't measure my success by other people's success, and that was the bottom line. Besides, I appreciate both Diana and Barbra as hard workers.

My son Clarence was a huge Diana Ross fan. He had so many pictures of her in his room his walls were covered. But then he started plastering Diana on the ceiling. I was amused but finally said, "Come on, Clarence, this is ridiculous." (Later he became a huge Chaka Khan fan.) When I went to see *Lady Sings the Blues,* I was interested to see whether girlfriend could pull it off. She did. My children and I also enjoyed *The Wiz,* although clearly Lena Horne stole the show.

I had ambitions to improve my presentation as a performer and my overall abilities as an artist. I've always been interested in improvement. This was when I enrolled at the Academy of Ballet. Ballet, in particular, has a grace and refinement I find appealing. If I hadn't been a singer, I might have been a prima ballerina and done arabesques with Arthur Mitchell, Alvin Ailey, or Rudolf Nureyev. At various times in the seventies, when I was slimmer and in especially good shape, I incorporated dance into my performance.

During another segment of my presentation, I also incorporated impressions of other singers. My ear and voice allow me to recreate the vocal idiosyncrasies of some of my colleagues. I got a big kick out of emulating Diana Ross doing "Ain't No Mountain High Enough," Gladys Knight's "Midnight Train to Georgia," Mavis Staples's "Let's Do It Again."

I was quite aware of what was happening in popular music during this period, just as I am aware of the scene today. I've always listened to the radio, watched TV, and kept up with the times. The times in the first half of the seventies were changing and getting increasingly funky. I'm talking about the dominance of a new wave that started back in the sixties with Ray Charles, James Brown, and

Sly Stone, exploded with George Clinton, and in the seventies segued into disco and Donna Summer.

Funk and disco were everywhere, and many feel my contributions—like "Respect," "Chain of Fools," "Rock Steady," "Ain't No Way," and "Angel"—helped to popularize the form and made it even more acceptable on a worldwide basis. Other producers in other cities were also adding to the mix. In Newark, New Jersey, a young man opened for me, doing a cover of the Temps' "I Can't Get Next to You." (The original, of course, was sung by the aforementioned Dennis Edwards.) In this new version, the singer slowed it down and wore it out. I found out his name was Al Green, and I wasn't surprised when he and his Memphis producer, Willie Mitchell, went on to burn up the charts with a soul sound that, all at once, was very old and very new.

A new sound was also coming out of Philly, where Kenny Gamble and Leon Huff were coming on strong with their superslick productions for Harold Melvin and the Blue Notes, featuring Teddy Pendergrass, maybe the most powerful soul singer since Marvin Gaye.

Meanwhile, Marvin had broken away from the Motown assembly line and was producing himself. "Let's Get It On," like "What's Going On" before it, proved Marvin was his own best producer. Same was true for Stevie Wonder, whose output in the seventies was unbelievable. Stevie came of age as a singer-writer-producer-arranger and great humanitarian. I always wanted to work with Stevie. However, Motown and Atlantic seemed to keep us at arm's length. A little later, though, Stevie sent me a song he wrote— "Until You Come Back to Me (That's What I'm Gonna Do)"— that became one of my bigger hits. Thanks a mill, Stevie.

I also had the pleasure of working with the Spinners, a group from Detroit I had known for years, and I got them on Atlantic

Records after their Motown contract expired. They teamed up with Gamble and Huff's partner Thom Bell and immediately scored in 1972 with "I'll Be Around" and "Could It Be I'm Falling in Love." Atlantic offered me no bonus or finder's fee for signing up a hit act. Though I was not aware of a finder's fee, I should and could have received one. Of course, the Spinners never looked back. But, thanks to Wolf going over to Atlantic and raising hell, Atlantic did agree to credit me as a coproducer on my own records. It was about time. Sometimes I wonder what would have happened if I had been a credited producer early on. I may well have had another career as a producer of other artists, soundtracks, commercials, and so on.

The first album on which I'm listed as coproducer is one many consider my finest. *Amazing Grace* is quite special. It's special because it took me back to the original source of my musical inspiration; it's also special because it reunited me with the man who had served as one of my first mentors. *Amazing Grace* took me back to church and to the King of Gospel, the Reverend James Cleveland.

When I say "took me back to church," I mean recording in church. I never left church. And never will. Church is as much a part of me as the air I breathe. I have heard people say that one singer or another "gave up gospel for pop." That is not my case. In 1960, when my father took me to Columbia, I expanded, but I never abandoned. I included other forms of music in my repertoire because of my love for all good music. Even today I continue to expand by learning semiclassical pieces and adding them to my program.

With that in mind, I told Atlantic that it was time for me to return to my roots and make a gospel album. They appreciated gospel and were pleased at my decision. I decided to travel to Los Angeles and record at the New Temple Missionary Baptist Church. Los Angeles was the home of James Cleveland, and James's Southern California Community Choir was one of the best anywhere. I wanted to make this record with James. No one could put together a choir like James Cleveland. It would be old home week, and I would be able to praise the Lord in the way to which I was accustomed. I brought in some of the musicians who had backed me on my secular records—Chuck Rainey on bass, Cornell Dupree on guitar, Bernard Purdie on drums. James played piano, and Ken Lupper played organ. Alex Hamilton, who was Lola Falana's accompanist, wrote the choir arrangements. I wanted this to be a live recording with a real congregation. Gospel is a living music, and it comes most alive during an actual service.

The preparations were intense. I got so busy and caught up in them that at some point my mentor Clara Ward, who would be an honored guest, reminded me that I had forgotten to invite my father! Oh no, how could I? I called him immediately, and naturally he was there. I asked him to speak. After hearing me sing, he told the congregation, "Aretha and James took me all the way back to the living room at home when she was six and seven years of age. I saw you crying . . . and I saw you respond . . . but I was just about to bust wide open . . . you talk about being moved. Not only because Aretha is my daughter, Aretha is just a stone singer . . . if you want to know the truth, she has never left the church." To be back in church—and back with Daddy and Clara and Clara's mother, Gertrude—was one of the greatest moments in my life.

We recorded on two separate nights, and on both nights the congregation was so spirited. It was everything I had hoped for—and more. I sang songs from my childhood—"Mary, Don't You

Weep," Clara Ward's "How I Got Over," and "Never Grow Old," which I first heard by Billy Kyles and the Thompson Community Choir of Chicago. James and I sang a duet on "Precious Memories." "Precious Memories" is what the service was all about. But I also wanted to include contemporary material. So I sang "Wholy Holy" from Marvin Gaye's *What's Going On* and, by making references to Jesus, put Carole King's "You've Got a Friend," a pop hit, into a gospel framework. It all worked. WLIB in New York and all of the gospel stations started playing it, and I heard it everywhere in the streets.

Miracle of miracles, it sold. The album went gold, and it was, I believe, the first gold LP in the history of gospel music. What pleased me even more was the fact that *Amazing Grace* served to spread gospel music to areas where it had never gone before. Gospel found new fans. Subsequently, I was also able to repay my great musical debt to James by giving his name to TV producers. And after that the Grammys presented artists like the Clark Sisters and Shirley Caesar to a vast mainstream audience. Along with Edwin Hawkins's "Oh Happy Day," *Amazing Grace* proved to the record industry that gospel could sell.

I would like to feel that I have made this contribution to gospel, from which I came. I was somewhat of a catalyst helping the secular musical world acknowledge and utilize gospel. And, of course, there was no holding gospel back anyway; there are far too many gifted artists, and it is too great a music; it was just a matter of time before it came into the prominence and popularity it so richly deserves. Black jocks began playing an occasional gospel song as part of their R&B programming. Producers like Quincy Jones, for example, started calling me to ask which gospel choirs to use on R&B and pop records. Over the years I've been delighted and happy to see the increasing acceptance of gospel. The Clark Sisters' "You

Brought the Sunshine" also began to get secular play and crossed over.

The *Amazing Grace* cover, as I mentioned, was shot by Wolf while we were at Sam Lord's castle in Barbados. My African-styled garb is an example of the fashions being designed by the New Breeders.

One last note about the album, which, unfortunately, is a negative one: My performances were filmed with no agreement with me in place. However, as of this writing I have been contacted about the possibility of it being in theaters this year or next or as a documentary. I believe I said God is good, and if a movie were meant to be, it would happen. The most interesting thing about it to me is *Amazing Grace* was my very first gold LP, and "Amazing Grace" may very possibly be my first full-length feature film in gospel for small art theaters. Would you say that there is a message there? When I saw what had been done in one section of the film, though, I was appalled: one of the cameramen kept shooting straight up underneath Clara's dress. She was in the front row. Talk about bad taste!

A sad note came a year later, in 1973, when my mentor died. Clara Ward was only forty-eight. She had called me just before she became ill, requesting that I write some things for her. Shortly thereafter my dad called to say he was flying out to L.A. to see her in the hospital. I felt she was trying to handle too many things as the lead singer, business manager, and booking agent for the Ward Singers.

Along with my dad, Miss Ward was my greatest influence. She was the ultimate gospel singer—dramatic, daring, exciting, courageous, and unarguably sincere in her love of the Lord. She took gospel where gospel had never gone before, introducing the form to the world beyond the black church. She was also my friend and supporter, a genuine person who had encouraged me at every stage of my career. Her funeral was held in Philadelphia. The mayor of the city spoke, along with other renowned ministers. Alex Bradford sang his famous "Too Close," and I sang "The Day Is Past and Gone," the same Clara Ward song I had sung as a child on my first gospel record. I loved her.

# Gotta Find Me an Angel

⟋

Nixon and the Vietnam War, Nixon and Watergate, televised hearings that went on forever. In the early seventies you couldn't turn on the TV without hearing another episode from the adventures of Tricky Dick. But the seventies were also about liberation— women's liberation and disco and *Saturday Night Fever.* I'm not a politician or political theorist. I don't make it a practice to put my politics into my music or social commentary. But the fact that "Respect" naturally became a battle cry and an anthem for a nation shows me something.

I was still in the throes of romance, still in love with Ken Cunningham. But there was always a slight undercurrent of conflict concerning my brother Cecil. Wolf questioned Cecil's managerial decisions from time to time, and I took offense. Cecil was a graduate cum laude from a distinguished college and a minister as well. He had the intellectual requirements to handle the job. And my attitude was, If his management wasn't bothering me, why would it bother Wolf? Wolf understood and, for a while, backed down.

Mr. Mystique was crossing my mind occasionally and, traveling the country, I would see him now and again, but nothing developed. I was committed to Wolf.

Just a few months after recording *Amazing Grace,* I returned to Los Angeles to start another major project, a record produced by Quincy Jones, *Hey Now Hey (The Other Side of the Sky).* The team of Aretha, Jerry Wexler, Arif Mardin, and Tommy Dowd had been going strong for over six years. This was my twelfth album for Atlantic, and I wanted a change. Q had worked with everyone from the Duke to the Count, not to mention Dinah and Sarah. He was a musician with a finely tuned jazz sensibility who was also embarking on R&B and pop. I appreciated his broadness and thought Q would be perfect. I asked for him, and he was perfect.

The record had a bit of a jazz edge, with songs like "Moody's Mood" and "Just Right Tonight." But I also contributed my own compositions—the title track, "Sister from Texas," and "Master of Eyes (The Deepness of Your Eyes)." And I couldn't resist covering Bobby Womack's "That's the Way I Feel About Cha."

It took a while to complete *Hey Now Hey,* but it was fun. Wolf and I enjoyed hanging out with Q, who was then married to Peggy Lipton of *The Mod Squad,* a popular TV show of the time. One night the four of us plus Richard Pryor and his lady were at Q's for dinner. It was a lovely evening until Richard reached over and slapped his lady. I looked up and thought, *I know he didn't just slap her.* But he had, and no one said anything. Okay! Moving right along . . . We were all in shock.

*Hey Now Hey* featured a controversial cover designed by Wolf and his friend Jimmy Dunn. Some people—including me—didn't like the presence of a hypodermic needle, although Wolf explained it as a symbol of the evils to be avoided. Anyway, I didn't get into that conversation and let Wolf work it out on his own.

The album wasn't a big seller, except for a single song that has proved to be one of my most enduring hits. Once again, Carolyn came up with gold, this time the beautiful, flowing, and melodic "Angel." I was so moved by the experience of first hearing the song, I decided to include some of our previous dialogue, which went like this: "I got a call the other day. It was my sister Carolyn, saying, 'Aretha, come by when you can, I got something that I want to say.' And when I got there, she said, 'You know, rather than go through a long drawn-out thing, I think the melody on the box will help me explain.' " Then I sang, "Gotta find me an angel . . . to fly away with . . . gotta find me an angel . . . who will set me free."

Carolyn had written soaring melodies before, but none soared higher than "Angel." The song had wings. It combined loneliness and hope in a way that spoke directly to the heart. "Angel" sold in excess of 900,000 copies and was about to hit a million records when Jerry Wexler told me to make a decision to continue promoting "Angel" or record "Bridge over Troubled Water" right away. The label explained if we didn't record and release "Bridge" then, it would be too late. Well, I had no idea "Angel" was so close to a million records, and I felt that, regardless of "Bridge," it seemed to be a hit and would go all the way. But some people felt "Bridge" was deliberately intended to stop the sale of "Angel" before one million. Truthfully, I cannot comment one way or the other. "Bridge" hit as well, but I've always regretted that "Angel" wasn't given a longer life. Tension developed between Q and Jerry Wexler. I'm afraid Quincy thought I could have been more supportive of him. I didn't realize what the problem was until long after it was over.

My live shows grew more exciting as I gained more confidence. I recall being backstage, getting ready to perform, when I heard my musicians and fans shouting out, "What it is . . . what it is"— a Claude Booker–coined catchphrase from the words to "Rock Steady," a monster hit. I savored the moment, the opening of my ultraglamorous engagement at the Coconut Grove in Los Angeles's Ambassador Hotel.

I had always dreamed of playing the Coconut Grove. There was such notoriety about it in musical history. Nancy Wilson had cut a live record there. And beyond that, I saw it as a vintage venue from the golden era of theatrical Hollywood and one of, if not the, last great Hollywood venues, a must to perform in.

I began the day by shopping Rodeo Drive, where, at Giorgio's, I spotted a gorgeous two-piece white satin gown with matching coat, jeweled buttons, and small mandarin collar. Minor alterations were needed, but I was assured all would be ready by show time. Meanwhile, I went back to the hotel to have my nails done. When I discovered that the manicurist was a lady from Detroit, it did my heart good. I savor hometown connections.

The outfit arrived at the hotel on schedule. I put it on and was floating on clouds. I truly felt like a queen. To make matters more special, my sisters, Erma and Carolyn, were singing with me that night. In their satin culottes of pastel peach and powder blue, they looked lovely. I've had many wonderful backup singers in my career, but there's nothing like the comfort and togetherness of having sisters by my side. After the show many Hollywood celebrities visited my dressing room—I recall Motown's Suzanne DePasse, Jim Brown, Diana Ross, and many others—and the evening remains a treasured memory.

Back in New York, my shows were growing more extravagant.

I was veering toward the spectacular. I was proud of my weight loss and feeling great about my figure. I was sometimes carried onstage by male dancers. I liked changing costumes during the show, going from something slinky and sexy to a sequined gown suggesting subtle sophistication. I produced the shows myself, and I developed a singular style.

I mentioned the song Stevie Wonder wrote for me, "Until You Come Back to Me (That's What I'm Gonna Do)." I cut it on *Let Me in Your Life,* the first studio Atlantic album for which I received—thank you, Jesus—coproducing credit. Released in 1974, *Let Me in Your Life* would be the last hit record I'd make with the Wexler-Mardin-Dowd team. Things were changing in the music business. New trends, like disco, were coming on strong. I enjoy new artists. I'm a progressive person. I'm also a traditionalist. I believe in the tradition of great music—solid songs, intelligent lyrics, superb accompaniment, and flawless production. That's how I was brought up, and that's how I maintain standards.

So when the producers Chuck Jackson and Marvin Yancy came to New York to present me with a smorgasbord of songs, I listened carefully. (Chuck, by the way, is the younger brother of Reverend Jesse Jackson. The Jacksons and Franklins have been friends for many years.) Finally, though, I didn't think the tunes met my requirements. They took some of the same songs—"This Will Be," "I've Got Love on My Mind"—to Natalie Cole and cut them with her. The songs hit, and Natalie was off to the races.

However, they say imitation is the highest form of flattery. In fact, when the Women of the Five Boroughs of New York honored me, she sang for me. I sent her flowers and welcomed her into the industry. But some industry magazines wanted to heat up the issue and sell some magazines. At one point Natalie called me to say that it was Chuck Jackson's idea—not hers—for her to try to sound like me. I considered that statement. Later, every time I opened a publication, it seemed like Natalie was telling journalists something about our fantasy feud. I refused to comment. I saw it as a way for Natalie to stay in the news and play on me. She also complained that I snubbed her and wouldn't communicate with her. Which wasn't true either—we had talked at least three or four times. So still I had nothing to say. Finally, my sister Erma called and said, "Aretha, why don't you just talk to her?" My reply was "Erma, if I want to be friendly with Natalie, I will be. And if I don't, I won't." I felt Natalie was out to create controversy and build her name by playing the innocent victim, and I wasn't about to buy into that, and I didn't.

Natalie later found her own style with more jazz-oriented material, and I enjoyed hearing who she really was as a singer. I wasn't interested in conducting a public dialogue with her about our relationship. And if there had been any real sincerity in her statements, she would have called me. When she did call me, she never intimated in any way that she was upset. As far as I was concerned, our relationship was cordial but incidental to the important things happening in my life. What *was* happening in my life?

During the disco craze, the program directors at radio stations were less likely to give veteran R&B acts a play. I liked some disco and thought that certain singers—Donna Summer, Gloria Gaynor—were well suited to the style. Later during the disco era, I met with Nile Rodgers and Bernard Edwards, whose group, Chic, was burning up the charts. They presented me with material that I liked. Good songs, in-the-pocket grooves, and cute lyrics. But when preproduction started, things cooled off in a hurry. Their idea for me was *Just come in and sing impromptu and we'll take it from there.* Well, I hadn't worked that way. I'm an interpreter, and I need to be involved with the total musical environment. I was game, but my relationship with Rodgers and Edwards ended before it began. There were unmentionables concerning their attitudes, which just didn't fly with me. They took those songs—"Upside Down" and "I'm Coming Out"—to Diana Ross. I had no regrets.

I take this business of soul music seriously; a song, like a person, must have a soul. I realized that my voice would have worked with disco tracks. But I was determined not to be labeled a disco artist. I'm in the music industry for the long run. No matter how much the radio stations were shoving rhythm and blues back in the corner, I still believed and I believe today in the permanent value and staying power of soul music. Soul music is cultural, and it should forever be enshrined as one of the world's greatest forms of music. It is a people, a nation, and it is the rhythm of our lives and loves and losses and wins, our hopes and dreams and passions on parade. Like jazz and gospel, it is a musical strain that will live forever because it is born out of real emotions and people's experiences. R&B isn't a fad; it's the truth.

It really was a shame how many traditional R&B artists suffered in the disco days. My record sales slumped only slightly at one point, even though later I would return to gold and platinum.

With any artist there are peaks and valleys. Just before disco dominated the airwaves, Atlantic knew it was time to change. Ahmet Ertegun gave me a list of hot producers. I selected Curtis Mayfield. And I'm glad I did, because together we put one of my favorite albums, *Sparkle,* on the market. It proved the permanent power of rootsy rhythm and blues. Mayfield, of course, was chief architect of the Impressions and composer-producer extraordinaire, the black Bach, as I called him. His soundtrack to

*Superfly* demonstrated still another aspect of his talent—making music for movies. *Sparkle* was a film that told the story of a girl group coming out of the neighborhood. I wanted to sing Curtis's suite of songs, but the project almost derailed before we got started.

Seems as though Mayfield had given the same set of songs to Carolyn. She called herself Baby Dynamite and had put out albums on RCA. Carolyn had also met with Mayfield. I knew none of this, and when I discovered what had happened, we were both upset. What the heck was he trying to do? It took Daddy's intervention to set things straight. It was decided that I would go to Chicago and she would work on another project. I did go to Mayfield's Curtom Studios in Chicago and embraced the music for several days.

Mayfield is a master of what I call sweet funk. Marvin Gaye had something of that same quality. The music is down, the grooves tight, the attitude real, and the overall feeling is loving and warm. Gentle. Tender. Caring. "Something He Can Feel," the hit single off *Sparkle,* is an example of that. Curtis is a producer-writer whose material inspires and immediately grabs you. His songs tell a beautiful story. *Sparkle* expressed the hopes and dreams of a young girl in the ghetto; Curtis captured a character whom I helped bring to life. I consider working with him—*Sparkle* and its follow-up, *Almighty Fire*—a highlight of my career.

In the mid-seventies my career took a spin. I watched much of the industry move east to west. Berry Gordy had been in California for years; Johnny Carson moved his show to L.A. The more I thought about it, the more I thought a change might be appropriate, and exciting. Ever since my dad and I drove through the Hollywood Hills during our gospel days, I found the city so charming and fairy-tale-like. Meanwhile, Wolf and I were having problems.

Maybe a change of scenery would help us all. Besides, the weather was gorgeous, the atmosphere laid-back, and I remembered over at Roscoe's House of Chicken & Waffles you could get a dynamite plate of a number of varieties of waffles.

Okay, L.A. We're on the way.

# *City of Angels*

I knew the city pretty well, starting with those days when Daddy and I came to L.A. for our gospel services at the Shrine Auditorium and stayed at the Watkins, followed by appearances at the 5-4 Ballroom. On recent trips I had stayed at the Beverly Hills Hotel, with its private bungalows, plush landscaped grounds, and whispers of a golden era gone by. I loved the bungalows. I also shopped the fabulous stores on Rodeo Drive and rode down Crenshaw Boulevard as it ran through the heart of the community, where I'd stop at Mr. Jim's Ribs, whose tag line was "You don't need no teeth to eat our meat."

Eventually I focused on Encino in the San Fernando Valley. It was less than a half-hour drive from Hollywood and Beverly Hills, and it provided the privacy I wanted for myself and my family. June Eckstine, Billy Eckstine's former wife, was the realtor who found the house on the corner of Rancho and Louise, adjacent to the Walt Disney estate. Mike Connors, star of *Mannix,* was a neighbor;

Marilyn McCoo and Billy Davis lived nearby. A few blocks over on Havenhurst was the Jackson family home. The Jacksons were another key reason I moved to Encino. I had hoped they and my sons might become friends, play basketball together, and relate to one another as young brothers. Our families made friendly overtures toward each other. As a matter of fact, I have a picture of a preteen Michael and Janet standing under a dwarf-sized tree in our backyard after a cooling swim. Janet and my son Clarence talked about it just before Janet's concert last year.

The house was two-story and ultracontemporary. A rippling brook, lined with dramatic boulders, ran right through the center of the property. I designed a rose walkway that extended from the curb to the front door, and the backyard was beautifully landscaped, complete with a pool. We had every reason to be happy, and God had more than blessed me to afford this beautiful home. Clarence, who had a fine musical ear, had moved from his Diana Ross phase into Chaka Khan. Eddie had a music group and was hanging out at Maverick Flats, a club that became the birthplace of acts like Shalamar with Howard Hewett. Eddie was also appearing on *Soul Train* as a dancer; in fact, he was the first *Soul Train* dancer to wear a suit and tie. Eddie also did a mean James Brown impression. Teddy was deep into rock. Ultimately he'd develop into a fine guitarist, graduating with degrees in telecommunications. And Kecalf, who'd later turn into a first-rate rapper and hip-hop producer, attended the Valley schools. Clarence dropped him off at the bus stop just a block away.

Along with my boys, I arrived in L.A. with Wolf and Stormin' Norman. Everyone loved Norm Dugger. He was big fun. Big Mama had told me early on, "You're not going to have more than three or four real true friends in your whole life." Well, Norman was sure enough one of them. When I met him, he was King Curtis's valet. After King's death he came to work for me as a road manager. Norman wore lots of hats. He was a million laughs. He could also get down in the kitchen, making a mean egg custard pie and killer homemade rolls. He was my main man all through the seventies and eighties.

Wolf continued to be a motivating force. Once in California I tended to hibernate in my suburban home. I was soooooooo comfortable with a Cancer moon; I got deep into domesticity. Some of the great things about L.A. are Pink's hot dogs down on LaBrea, not to mention burgers at Tommy's and Fatburger. Wolf would warn me. He'd point out that many of my colleagues were busy getting in shape, saying that Stephanie Mills was running in Central Park and Diana Ross was working out with Nautilus equipment. But I was still reluctant to get moving and really didn't feel I needed it. Until . . .

I went to Pittsburgh to perform. I was feeling okay. But then, halfway into the concert, I suddenly found myself out of breath. For a singer, that's serious. Alarming. Not to mention embarrassing. If your breath isn't there, you can't sustain and perform properly. I immediately knew that Wolf was right—I was badly out of shape. And I vowed to make a change.

I turned to dance, one of my original passions, and asked the New York Academy of Ballet, where I had taken instruction, to recommend someone in L.A. They mentioned Stephen Wenta. He proved to be a blessing. I enrolled in Wenta's ballet classes and, over a period of time, regained my strength and stamina. My couch potato days were over.

During this same period of time, Wolf and I were still having slight problems. The love between us was alive, but our conflict

over Cecil was escalating. I felt pressure when Wolf questioned Cecil's managerial decisions. If I liked the way Cecil took care of my business, that should have been enough for Wolf. But Wolf had a mind of his own. I respected his positive comments and qualities but wouldn't allow anything or anyone to weaken the bond between me and my brother.

Besides the personal issues between us, Wolf loved New York and, once he saw I was settled in L.A., moved back to Manhattan, where he took acting lessons at Lee Strasberg's Actors Studio. Our romantic relationship ended, but our friendship and our respect for each other did not. Wolf has remarried, has four adorable children, and lives in Washington, D.C. In the memory of my heart, he remains one of the most real and caring men I have ever known.

Dennis reappeared on the set. We dated again, but only in my lightly and slightly mode. I heard from a reliable source that he was still shuffling his women, but I was still naïve enough to think he was on the real side. The straw that broke the camel's back was an incident at the Beverly Comstock Hotel. Dennis had come to L.A. We had plans to meet. (It never happened.) When Dennis turned on the charm, he turned it on full force.

For all of his dealing out of different bags, there was no denying his talent. That point was brought home to me on a night that the Temptations reunited for a concert at the Greek Theater. It was a beautiful and balmy California evening that turned red-hot once the Temps hit the stage. The stars were in the sky and the stars were onstage. Two stars in particular lit up the night—Dennis and the man he had once replaced, David Ruffin. They went after each other, trading songs—"Ain't Too Proud to Beg," "My Girl," "Papa Was a Rollin' Stone," "Psychedelic Shack," "I Wish It Would

Rain," "Runaway Child, Running Wild"—trading licks, bending notes, running through riffs. Incredible. I was on the edge of my seat all evening and was in and out of my chair. Neither David nor Dennis would give an inch. It was a musical triumph for them and sheer joy for the audience. I was witnessing two of the best male soul singers in the galaxy putting on a show I would never forget.

Another unforgettable show was my appearance at the Hollywood Bowl. Prior to the concert, James Cleveland had his man Elbert fry up a lot of the gospel bird, ham hocks and greens, fried corn—a soul buffet extraordinaire. (After leaving James, Elbert became cook to Diana Ross. And Elbert beat Nautilus, filling out her Twiggy-like frame.) At the Bowl, James and his entire church were in the front rows. Sugar Ray Robinson was in the wings, about three feet away from me, but I didn't make a point of speaking to him. I regret it, as I was one of the greatest fight fans. We never seemed to be in the same place at the same time.

After the Bowl concert, I was invited to Berry Gordy's mansion in Bel Air. This was a real treat for me and the group. We drove up a narrow road that wound around the side of a mountain. James Bond had to step back and give it up; Berry had the upper hand. There was a checkpoint with security men in dark glasses before we drove at least another half a mile to reach the house.

Berry took me on a tour. The grounds were incredible— the exquisite aviary, the peacocks on parade, the manicured gardens. In the master bedroom and his private quarters, he pointed to two portraits done on black velvet, one of Diana Ross—no surprise there—and one of *myself*—big surprise! I was flattered. I had no idea Berry appreciated me to such a degree. In addition to the music, perhaps he's sentimental and appreciates the old and early days, when we all were just starting out to realize our dreams.

With Wolf back in New York and Dennis and me not dating, I was free from attachments. This was the mid-seventies. Mr. Mystique and I indulged in a few midnight conversations, and the coals were still smoldering. I saw him once or twice and wanted very much to spend some time with him, but he was moving fast and I didn't want a one-night affair, so Ma Bell got the best of our interactions.

As America moved deeper into its love affair with disco, my record sales stayed slightly off. I tried new producers and hired some of the biggest names in the business—Lamont Dozier (of the famed Holland-Dozier-Holland team, architects of the Supremes' sound), Marvin Hamlisch and Carole Bayer Sager, Marty and David Paich. *Sweet Passion* was the name of the album, and it was inspired by Mr. Mystique and our first real encounter, when he missed his plane in New York. I still cherished the memory: I had never been kissed, touched, or loved like that. I had never been to a hotel with a man at his invitation, and waiting for him to get the room at the front desk, I felt a little cheap. But the event that followed quickly overshadowed that.

Meanwhile, for a time I turned my attention to fashion. My dream was to establish a line of Aretha Franklin creations in connection with a name designer. I took my sketches to Willie Smith in New York, and we had some good discussions. But Willie didn't want to risk his hard-earned security in the industry by taking a chance on my designs. Back in L.A., I contacted Steven Burrows. When it came to women's clothes, Burrows was highly respected, and I thought he and I would make a good match. Unfortunately, those discussions never got off the ground. The

Aretha Franklin line of design is still yet to be born. But stay tuned . . .

Even during the disco days, my profile was still relatively high. I performed at the Oscars several times and once, I recall, sang a duet with Frankie Laine, the singer from the fifties who had a big hit with "Mule Train." It was very exciting. I was especially thrilled because, much to my surprise, my dad was in attendance. I hadn't seen Daddy in over a year. When I saw him and we hugged, I started crying. "What's wrong, Ree?" he asked with concern. "I just haven't seen you in so long," I answered. "I've missed you." I had been so caught up in concerts and recordings, although we always talked long-distance.

In 1976 I was pleased that Jimmy Carter was elected president. It was about time a Democrat got back in there. I sang at the pre-inaugural concert. Shirley MacLaine was there along with her brother, Warren Beatty. And I noticed that when I sang "Rock with Me" off the *Sparkle* album, Carter stood up and did a little finger-poppin' and light boogying of his own. He was really very down and regular. Later that night I met Bette Davis, and we exchanged Aries credentials. She said, "You and I know something, don't we?" I said, "Right," and we both started laughing. Bette was cool, and we could talk.

My father was also in attendance. After the event my feet were terrifically swollen. I had been on them all day, running around and rehearsing. I spotted Daddy coming up the hallway and wanted to take him back to meet the president. But it was the president or my feet; my spirit was willing, but my feet weren't. I felt like I was walking on soft-boiled eggs. I felt bad until I learned later that Daddy had already met President Carter and could have introduced me to him.

Aside from the excitement of public events, my life was relatively calm, relaxed and growing. I was into my laid-back California lifestyle, tending my vegetable garden and flowers, watching the kids grow up, dealing with the rigors of parenting and children, and following my favorite soaps on TV. What transpired next was totally unexpected. Marriage was the last thing on my mind.

# Here Comes the Bride

Los Angeles was not the easiest time in my life. Cecil was back in Detroit, and I needed representation—a booking agent—on the West Coast to supplement my brother's effort. Ruthie Bowen of Queen Booking and I were having our problems. She had over-committed me by one date, knowing my limitations, to an English promoter for a long tour of Great Britain that I ultimately rejected. The result was a suit against me and not her.

Cecil and I initiated several meetings with bookings agencies. I met with some big names, like Jerry Weintraub, who invited me to his office for a catered lunch. The food was good, but the meeting ended when Weintraub said it was a bad idea for me to have my own TV special. For a while I signed with ICM. They found me lucrative work doing commercials. I sang for the Yellow Pages, Armour hot dogs, and "Diamonds Are Forever," all products I liked. Ultimately, though, I was a recording artist, not a commercial artist, and, despite my earnings, I still felt my career was dormant.

The condition of my love life, though, was about to be a completely different story. Rosey Grier had a benefit banquet for the charity program he called Giant Step. I was happy to contribute my performance, not knowing that my romantic life was about to take a Giant Step of its own. While I was in my dressing room, my son Clarence was roaming around gathering autographs when he ran into Glynn Turman, the actor. "My mother likes your work," Clarence told Glynn. He spoke the truth. I knew many of Glynn's films and was especially fond of *Five on the Black Hand Side.* He was also one of the stars of *Cooley High.*

Clarence brought Glynn to my dressing room. We exchanged small pleasantries and swapped phone numbers. My afterglow feelings were . . . mmmmm . . . very interesting . . .

Days passed. I was getting my hair done at Salon Jopet, talking to my friend and operator Clifford Peterson, a celebrated Hollywood stylist. Clifford was laughing and screaming about how all the Hollywood starlets were after Glynn. And shortly thereafter, Glynn began to call. On our first date he came to the Valley, where we went out to eat. I was interested and lightly excited. He was a man of varied interests and keen intellect. He was extremely serious about his acting and craft. He also loved horses and riding—he and his uncle owned a ranch outside L.A.—and favored western hats. He knew a great deal about the history of black cowboys. I was also pleased to learn he loved jazz and seemed to be an Aretha Franklin fan. Our date went well until he said something that threw me for a loop. "I would like to be friends," he announced, "but I'm really not interested in a relationship." "Neither am I," I said, thinking, *I didn't invite him to lunch.*

Carolyn was having some problems in her apartment, and someone had tried to break in on her. I told her to get her things and come on over and stay with me. Carolyn was basically an optimist with lots of energy. I was lying across the bed, and all of a sudden

I thought, *Hey, I'm not staying in tonight. Tonight's the premiere of* The Greatest, *Muhammad Ali's movie.* I asked Carolyn, "Do you want to go?" "Absolutely" was her response. And we started dashing about and getting dressed to the nines.

We went, and we loved it. It was all too glamorous. To see Ali's heroics portrayed on the big screen was a thrill. It brought back vivid memories of the Greatest's greatest fights. At a time when the popular culture portrayed far too few black heroes, I was delighted to see Ali get his due. The soundtrack was dynamite. We boogied at the after-party, and the girl who played Belinda threw down so bad she was totally believable.

Glynn was a lot more interested than he first let on. Later I learned that Ben Vereen, one of his close friends, told him right off the top, "Invite me to the wedding." Meanwhile, Glynn called me for another date, and then another, and then another. The more I got to know Glynn, the more I liked him. I could tell he was a giving man with a sharp sense of humor. I liked his quiet manner and his appreciation for his fellow artists. Among his closest friends were equally serious thespians like Louis Gossett, Jr.

Glynn had two boys and a girl, and of course I had my four boys, so dating was not easy. But somehow we managed. He had a house in Santa Monica, and we spent many lovely evenings at the beach dining by candlelight while we gazed at golden sunsets and the rippling tides washing ashore. There's nothing quite like a California sunset to set the mood for a blossoming romance. And the cool breeze and smell of the ocean appropriately contributed to the whole. Over time, our romance deepened. Glynn moved from his original position to a more, shall we say, hands-on approach.

All our dates had been in the L.A. area—soul concerts at the Greek or Universal, dining at the Hungry Tiger or Roscoe's House of Chicken & Waffles, or barbecue from Mr. Jim's or Leo's, or often I would cook. I felt we were headed in a more serious direction when Glynn invited me to accompany him to Texas, where he was working in a play. I accepted. I remember it being very cold. I remember Glynn wearing red B.V.D.'s and jeans, which I thought were kind of cute. And of course I remember his poppin' the question. We were sitting on the bed, talking, when he just came out and asked me. I was floored, but after two or three minutes, I looked him in the eyes and said, "Yes."

The first person I told was Daddy, who was concerned, as any parent would be. He said, "But you've only known him a year and a half. Why not wait another year?" A year was too long. Six months was more like it. And six months would give me time to plan the kind of spectacular wedding I had long dreamed of. I recognized the wisdom of Daddy's words, but this new love was so engaging.

The preparations were special. I wanted this to be the wedding of weddings, and this time my father was going to marry me. This time I wanted to be married in the church of my childhood, the church where I grew up, learning to sing and accept Jesus Christ as my personal Savior. I wanted to be married in New Bethel Baptist Church, 8450 C. L. Franklin Boulevard, as it is known now, Daddy's church. I cannot go there without thinking of him and his many sermons and hearing his voice of Sundays past.

Glynn agreed to a Detroit wedding and, for our Hollywood friends, a Beverly Hills reception the day after. Two cities, two separate celebrations, no expense spared. I also thought it fair to have a prenuptial agreement. One was prepared, stipulating that all we had earned and acquired before the marriage would be considered separate property.

The day before the wedding Glynn and I checked into the Michigan Inn off the Lodge Freeway on J. L. Hudson Drive in Detroit, which is where I gave him a copy of the prenuptial. In the morning, when I asked him if he had signed it, he said it was missing. He just didn't know where it was. Maybe the maid took it. I called my lawyer and said I needed another copy. He promised to have it in Detroit before the ceremony began.

The day of the wedding—April 11, 1978—I was thrilled and as happy as any blushing bride could be, but concerned on the back burner about the missing prenuptial agreement. Crowds had lined up outside the church early that morning, and people were standing on the tops of buildings to get a glimpse. Photographers from national magazines, from *Ebony* to *Time,* were already waiting. When I arrived at the church in the afternoon, I was flanked by a number of security men. I was startled by the fans chanting my name—"Aretha, Aretha"—over and over, reaching out for a handshake or autograph. Sometimes you forget you're a celebrity, and my mind was a million miles away from the stage. For some reason I had expected it to be much quieter. The crowd was extremely intense. And after struggling to get into the church, I was almost in tears. We were escorted to the pastor's study, where I sat and composed myself and finally asked about the prenuptial papers. Had they arrived? No, they had not. I couldn't help but wonder if I would go ahead with the ceremony without a signed agreement.

One hour before the ceremony they still had not arrived. As I sat waiting, Monetta Sleet of *Ebony* magazine danced from one end of the church to the other, snapping pictures of every moment. Still no agreement. Then, with ten minutes to go, someone came running through the front door with the express envelope. The second prenuptial had finally arrived and was hand-carried to

Glynn. He signed. Thank God I didn't have to decide what to do if he hadn't.

I married Glynn Turman, dashing bridegroom and distinguished actor. The church of my childhood, moved to a new location but the church nonetheless, was splendid. I wore a silk gown trimmed in mink and adorned with thousands of tiny pearls. The train was eight feet long and made by Ruthie West of Los Angeles. My father presided, and the Four Tops sang Stevie Wonder's "Isn't She Lovely." I have never felt more beautiful. Lou Gossett was the best man and Erma my maid of honor. There were eight bridesmaids and eight groomsmen. Carolyn sang a composition she had written especially for the occasion, a beautiful song called "I Take This Walk with Thee." The choir sang the hymns I had loved as a little girl. The church elders were in attendance and people I had known my whole life. My sisters and brothers, Big Mama, my children, and Glynn's children—everyone who was near and dear to me. Cousin Brenda also sang. It was all so exquisite.

The highlight of the reception was cutting the eight-foot, four-tier wedding cake amid the popping of flashbulbs and cheering of the guests. Then we flew back to L.A. and another wedding party. We had invited five hundred guests to the ultraswank affair at the Beverly Hilton, with food by Milton Williams, the world-famous Beverly Hills caterer. When it was all over, I was too exhausted but very happy. In addition to the festivities, one of the bridesmaids tried to upstage the reception by dressing to the height in her catch clothes, a see-what-I-had-for-lunch dress (all see-through).

∽

Meanwhile, back at the ranch, the radio jocks and program directors were playing the disco divas while many soul artists were being phased out. After going back and forth with ICM, I switched over to William Morris, where Dick Alen, a veteran who had been booking soul artists like Chuck Berry and Solomon Burke, began booking me. I like Dick because he understands me, and I appreciate his considerable skills. Dick is great. We're still together today, although we have had a day or two that weren't exactly strawberries and cream.

Back at Atlantic Records, things were somewhat quiet. My records were falling short of the mark for gold. I began to feel that the label's promotion and marketing were not creative enough and wondered whether a change was in order. Meanwhile, reading *Billboard* magazine, the music industry bible, I noticed how Barry Manilow's career had taken off in a most dramatic fashion. But more than being impressed by his big hits—songs like "I Write the Songs" and "Copacabana"—I saw the skillful publicity and promotional layouts that had preceded his success; I liked the way his career was being constructed. Dionne Warwick and Melissa Manchester were on the same label, Arista, headed by CEO Clive Davis, a music-business veteran and former chief of Columbia Records, my first label. Clive got in touch with me long-distance, and he flew out to the coast for this auspicious occasion.

I didn't know Clive when we were at Columbia. That's where he had ushered the label into the era of hard rock and soul back in the sixties by signing people like Janis Joplin, Sly and the Family Stone, and Earth, Wind & Fire. But Arista was his own label, which he had started from scratch; Arista was Clive's baby. During our initial get-together, I found him to be a man of keen intellect and savoir faire and a bon vivant, seasoned arbiter of good taste.

By then Jerry Wexler had left Atlantic and my main contact was Ahmet Ertegun. Naturally I would talk to Ahmet before making any decision. After all, I had been with Atlantic for over a decade. It was at Atlantic where I made and enjoyed lasting friendships, where my classic hits were cut, and where my career took such a dramatic turn. I will always be grateful to Ahmet, Jerry, Arif Mardin, and Tommy Dowd, my recording team, for being the launching pad that put into orbit a work that is still circling the globe.

I invited Ahmet and Noreen Woods, his executive vice president, to my home to discuss a new contract, and I prepared a beautiful dinner and served caviar over ice, but Ahmet was looking for down-home cooking. He said he could get caviar anywhere; he wanted some serious soul food. So I stepped up the pièce de résistance, served him some of my Shrimp à la Ree, and watched him eat to his heart's content.

The evening was fun, Ahmet serving up stories of the old days at Atlantic with Joe Turner, Ray Charles, LaVern Baker, and Ruth Brown. Not only did I like hearing about the heroes and heroines of rhythm and blues but I respected the manner in which Ahmet continued to support certain artists in need, even after they were off the label. When it came time to discuss business, the conversation was brief and to the point: Ahmet made it clear he wanted me to stay on Atlantic, and he made an offer to renew my contract. I said that Cecil and I would take it under consideration.

Meanwhile, Glynn and I were setting up house, even as our careers were heading in different directions. My cash flow was not flowing in the way that it should have. With a big gig coming up in Las Vegas, my wardrobe was not what it should have been. I had been giving most of my attention to the first years of my marriage. I've always had the most beautiful gowns in the world and didn't want to start compromising my appearance. I called my father for a loan. This was the first and only time he had sent me anything since I left home. Without hesitating, he sent me five thousand dollars and a telegram that said, "I'll see you in Las Vegas at your opening," scheduled for the Aladdin Hotel in 1979. They were the last words my father ever wrote me.

# Today I Sing
## the Blues

~

It was among the first secular songs I ever recorded. "Today I Sing the Blues" was a good song because it was real. On any given day, any of us can have the blues. We don't control fate or destiny, and we can't always control the circumstances of our lives. We don't control when, where, and why tragedy befalls us.

The end of the seventies was just the beginning of trying times. I didn't see it then, but, looking back, I see it now. The end of the seventies and much of the eighties would be the most challenging period of my life. Yet among those challenges were tremendous blessings and beautiful successes. In many ways, it would be a time of intense emotions.

Glynn was an intense artist. He came out of several distinguished Negro ensemble companies and had a strong sense of the skill and subtleties of great acting. He was also an acting teacher. In fact, he gave lessons in downtown L.A., where I had a standing invitation to sit and observe. I was especially interested because I had been offered a nice role in *The Blues Brothers,* the comedy film with John

Belushi and Dan Aykroyd. Glynn was an intelligent and generous instructor, but his classes were not my cup of tea. He was big on encouraging everyone to lose their inhibitions by yelling and screaming. That was Glynn's way of loosening up the class. I could certainly yell and scream, but not for just any reason at all. Although I understood his approach, I wasn't up for getting on the wild. It just was not my style. He also had us describing objects—a pen, a photograph, a ring—as they were passed around the room. The idea was to sharpen our perceptions. It was interesting to see how, as the objects went from one student to another, descriptions were voiced. Interesting, but not interesting enough to keep me in class.

Yet when it was time to shoot my scene in *The Blues Brothers,* I was relaxed and ready to go. I played the part of a loving but agitated wife whose husband is about to abandon her for the Blues Brothers band. In an extended cameo, I got several meaty lines and sang the full version of "Think," my big hit from 1968. Now, eleven years later, the song sounded better than ever. The movie was a smash. In addition to Dan, John, and me, the stars included Cab Calloway, Ray Charles, and James Brown. I was delighted to read that my reviews were universally positive.

For all the good days Glynn and I shared, there were a few bumps in the road. I remember one day when the vibe turned bad. I was expected in Hollywood for an *Essence* magazine photo shoot. Earlier that day Glynn and I had been arguing. As we were about to leave for the shoot, I looked down at the front door, where we were standing, and saw that Glynn had not put his shoes on. I decided I would not ask him why, and we left. When it was time to drive from Encino to Hollywood, he got behind the wheel of my chocolate Fiat sports car while I rode shotgun. The way Glynn was racing up the Hollywood Freeway, we could have had a terrible accident. I was upset, he was furious, and he took it out on the road. He was tailgating at sixty, seventy, eighty miles an hour.

"This is some shit I don't play!" I let him know in no uncertain terms. "Glynn, you are driving too fast. If you want to drive that fast, that's your business. But not with me in the car."

He slowed down, and we arrived at the shoot, put on our best faces, and somehow made it through the day. But our feelings remained bruised.

Without a word of warning came the fateful night at the Aladdin Hotel in Las Vegas. It was June 1979. I remember that H. B. Barnum was my conductor. During rehearsals Glynn and Cecil were at the foot of the stage, both advising me that a design I was wearing really wasn't happening. From the audience's point of view you could see straight up it and tell what I had for breakfast that morning. I decided they were right, and I changed.

We arrived later that evening for the first show. I was just completing the performance, having sung Earth, Wind & Fire's "Boogie Wonderland," when I saw Cecil and Glynn in the wings. I finished the last song and walked toward them. Cecil put his arms around me and told me that Daddy had been shot. *Oh my God.* I felt myself reeling but managed to make it to the dressing room, where we all went into prayer. In a frenzy of calls, we phoned the hospital and then the airport, trying to get on the first flight to Detroit. Telephones were ringing in every room. One caller was Pops Staples, whom I had known ever since I was a young girl. "Aretha," he said, "I'm sorry to be the one to have to tell you this, but your father is dead." Fear and disbelief gripped my heart.

At that moment, the world stopped. I firmly responded, "That isn't true. I just spoke to the hospital, and they have assured me that he is still alive and they're doing everything that they can to keep him comfortable." "I'm sorry, Aretha," said Pops, "but radio stations all over are reporting his death. I'm afraid it's true." I ignored Pops, hung up, and went with the hospital report. Thank God I didn't have a weak heart, because Pops Staples's initial false report could have done me in. His daughter Mavis had called Carolyn, telling her a similar thing, but at least with a degree of sensitivity.

The Detroit papers reported that burglars had entered our home on LaSalle and, in the course of a robbery, shot my father in the knee and groin. After hearing shots and seeing people running down the driveway, members of a religious brotherhood who lived directly across the street went to the back of the house and climbed through the second-floor window, where they discovered my father wounded. They summoned an ambulance. My sister Erma was called to the hospital to make the identification. When Big Mama heard the news, she collapsed. Ultimately, the men were found, tried, and convicted relatively quickly. But that didn't help my father.

I got to Detroit as soon as possible. Daddy had fallen into a coma. He would remain in what they call a light coma—because he required no life-sustaining mechanism—for the next five years. At various times we were given various prognoses. We didn't know whether he'd ever be able to speak or move on his own again. For years there was nothing, no sign of consciousness. Dr. Claude Young, our family physician, said that Daddy could come back at any time. And one evening he seemed to be doing just that; for a few moments I believed he was conscious. In his eye-to-eye contact with me he seemed to be saying, *I don't know why.* I was sad but encouraged when I saw this. He even shrugged his shoulders. Then he lapsed back into the same state. From the time he was shot to the day he died, my father would never communicate with us again.

The emotional consequences were devastating for all of us. Daddy was not only our father; since the death of our mom in 1952, he had also been our mother. He had been our everything. A man of enormous energy and boundless vitality, a man of high eloquence and burning intellect, he was now without speech or the ability to move. He was Daddy, and we kept him as best we could, as best money could afford. Erma engaged and I approved three practical nurses, doing around-the-clock shifts of eight hours each.

Carolyn, who had been living with me in Encino, was the first to move home to help Erma and Cecil care for Daddy. I essentially lived between the cities, Los Angeles and Detroit, flying back and forth every month. A difficult chapter—perhaps the most difficult of my life—had opened. Only my faith in God got me through.

With all this in mind, I couldn't ignore my career. I needed money for Daddy. I felt that no one would promote me with the enthusiasm and skill of Clive Davis. Naturally I consulted Cecil, who agreed that a change was in order. These were nervous times, which is probably why both Cecil and I were smoking too much, about two packs a day each, and I was going into three. But some were just in the ashtray and were my saving grace. Yet we both were coughing badly from smoking, and I told Cecil I was changing my brand and backing off cigarettes. Nothing has ever been harder in my life.

During all this, Clive was reassuring. He had an ear for hits, and he also offered me something I had been missing since Jerry Wexler had left Atlantic—personal involvement. Unlike Jerry, Clive didn't come to the studio. Jerry was a hands-on producer; Clive was and wasn't, certainly not to the extent he felt it necessary to be in the studio with me. He trusted my judgment and many years of experience. But Clive certainly was involved in all other aspects of the recording. We spent hours discussing the right producers and right songs.

I wanted a hit, and I also wanted to tap the rich resources of my past. That's why Clive and I agreed on Arif Mardin, the sensitive and brilliant arranger from my early Atlantic days, to produce four of the songs. One of them, "Come to Me," was a pretty popular record. For the other material, I used Chuck Jackson as producer. As a longtime friend and proven talent, Chuck understood where I wanted to go musically. At that point he was no longer working with Natalie Cole and was free to give me his full attention. The result was a modest hit, "United Together," the song that got the ball rolling at Arista.

We called the album simply *Aretha.* In addition to Chuck and Arif, I brought back some friends like Cissy Houston, who reunited the Sweet Inspirations for my background vocals. On some tracks we had veterans from my Atlantic days like Richard Tee, Cornell Dupree, and Fathead Newman. On others I was surrounded by new friends, like David Foster and the guys from Toto, an extremely hot group in the early eighties that included David Paich, son of the extraordinarily gifted writer Marty Paich. David was fondly called the Prince of Hog. I wrote and coproduced one of the tunes, "School Days," and couldn't resist covering the Doobie Brothers' sensational "What a Fool Believes," which had been sung so soulfully by Michael McDonald.

Not to forget the glories of the rich history of rhythm and blues, I cut an updated, kick-the-ballistics version of Otis Redding's "Can't Turn You Loose," a gem from the sixties that garnered me a 1980 Grammy nomination. All in all, I was pleased to be back in the groove. I especially loved the gorgeous album cover shot by Harry Langdon, famed photographer to the Hollywood film stars.

My life was compartmentalized. There was my career, and there was my family. My family obligation centered on being there for Daddy. Being there was not easy for any of us. You sat with him and you hoped he was comforted by your presence and knew you were there, but you didn't know. You also came to know who your and his true friends were. Big Mama's words of wisdom came back to me. You would be able to count your real, true friends, not associates or colleagues, on one hand. Jesse Jackson was a steadfast source of strength. He visited whenever he came to town. And Reverend Jim Holley stood around Daddy's bedside with us and prayed as we joined hands. True friends offered their hearts, their time, and their love.

Reverend Billy Kyles from Memphis, on whom I had my first childhood crush, proved to be another solid friend and supporter. Billy came to Detroit many times over the course of Daddy's debilitation to preach for Ben Hooks at Greater New Mount Mariah. I cooked dinner for Billy, and we had a lovely afternoon just talking over Shrimp à la Ree and rice. Katherine, who had been Daddy's housekeeper and cook for many years, finally came. For a long while she had been afraid she wouldn't be able to tolerate seeing my dad comatose and incapacitated. But she was amazed at how good he looked, saying how she wished she had come sooner. We saw none of the regulars who had been around for all of the good times. A certain minister whom Daddy introduced to the church and the city eventually went on to get his own church after trying to take Daddy's in his misfortune and absence.

# "You've Got to Hold On"

It was so hard for me to walk away from our house on LaSalle, to walk away from my dad and go back to work. But I had no choice. I had a concert in L.A. at the Greek Theatre, which, God knows, I wanted to cancel. It was the last place I wanted to be; I wanted to be by Daddy's bedside. However, Daddy required licensed practical nurses twenty-four hours a day, seven days a week. The insurance paid only 80 percent of his hospital bills, and the nurses' bills alone were over fifteen hundred dollars a week. I learned a serious people lesson from that time. Where were the people who were on Daddy's personal payroll and whom he had hosted all those years? Some of his closest associates wrote him off quicker than you could bat your eye; within months they had thrown their support behind the new acting minister, never giving Daddy time to recover.

On one of my dozens of plane trips from Detroit to L.A., I was doing all right until, walking through the airport with my security people, Bill Jackson and Frank Price, I stopped to buy some magazines at the newsstand. I caught a glimpse of a headline from the

Michigan *Chronicle,* C. L. FRANKLIN GRAVE. Seeing those words in black and white stunned me. I was devastated throughout my soul. I began to cry and doubled over walking to the gate, B.J. and Frank, who were more than just security people—they were friends as well—were as comforting as possible.

I never talked about it, not with the public and not in interviews. There was no way I could express the pain. I merely went on. At one point family friction escalated sharply. Glynn and I were in Detroit for one of my monthly visits. We were staying at Cecil's when we were called to Erma's, where Carolyn and Cecil were in a terrible fight over who would get to keep Daddy's car. I feel his car was just a way for each of them to be close to Daddy, and everybody's nerves were raw. I was on my way to intervene when Glynn convinced me to let him go instead. He felt the situation would be too upsetting for me and, given his good relationship with Cecil, he might be able to settle the matter quickly. I said okay. He did it, and everyone settled down. I appreciated Glynn cooling things out.

My finances were still under repair. I needed a significant amount of money with my monthly expenses and Daddy's medical care. I felt that Atlantic still owed me considerable old royalties and started putting in phone calls to them, but to no avail. At one point, upset about my father and the mounting pressure from all sides, I shouted over the phone to whomever I was speaking—as I recall, it was someone in business affairs—that I wanted my money and I wanted it now. I was at the top of my voice, sounding unlike anything you've ever heard from me onstage or on a record. I felt Atlantic owed me. Then the label did something I considered so low-class and tacky: they went public with my accounting statements, trying to prove they didn't owe me anything. Well, I'm sorry, I didn't agree with them, and they did not prove the point.

Meanwhile, in the early eighties, my career was making demands that I felt obligated to meet. I had, after all, switched to a new label and was going to gladly honor the commitment that Clive and his staff had made to me. I agreed to certain selected concert dates and a trip to England. England represented a particular challenge. I mentioned how some years earlier a slated tour of Great Britain had resulted in a misunderstanding between me and my agent Ruthie Bowen. She was the one who had overcommitted me, but people will go after whomever they think they can get the money from, not who is right or who is wrong. When I finally found the time and schedule that suited me, I was off to England.

Nevertheless, London was mellow. At noon, when everything stops in London, I liked hearing the clocks strike their delicate tones. The afternoons brought the delightful English custom of teatime. Teddy and I enjoyed it all—the scones with the best Devonshire cream and strawberry jam. Despite earlier events, the tour was a smashing success.

The opening date was the most spectacular. Sammy Davis, Jr., was the host of a gala command performance in London attended by Prince Charles and the Queen Mother. It was a moving night. I could hear the words my father had spoken to me when I was a child: "One day you will sing for kings and queens." That day had arrived.

That was the night I wore my first Jean Louis gown. He was the man who designed the Sandra Dee wardrobe I had admired as a teenager. Before my trip I went to Beverly Hills and met with him, spoke a little French, to his surprise, and told him what I had in mind. His design was simple, beautiful, white chiffon lightly beaded with sequins with a nude soufflé in the center. To maintain the simplicity of the style, I wore no jewelry.

My makeup lady, Regina Lynche, jokingly said that as I sang

"Amazing Grace" the Queen Mum's crown tilted to the side. She was rocking to the music. After the performance she and Prince Charles came to greet us. Lady Di, not yet married to Charles, was also there. I chatted with the Royal Family and found them surprisingly down-to-earth and easy to be with.

I went home and returned to the studio, wanting to maintain the momentum of *Aretha,* my first Arista album. The reunion with Arif Mardin had gone so well that I decided to go for one more. With a little coproduction from yours truly, Arif put together *Love All the Hurt Away.* The title song was a groove. I had long loved the guitar and vocal work of George Benson. The brother can play and sing. Clive and I thought a duet with George might be just enough newness to interest both our fans. We got together round midnight in the studio. The lights were low and the vibes were right. We sang. The duet was wonderfully received. Occasionally in concert I sang my part as well as a kicked-back impersonation of George. The audience loved it.

*Love All the Hurt Away* also featured one of my favorites, "It's My Turn," written by Michael Masser. Diana Ross had it done earlier, but, as the song says, it was my turn. The song had been a favorite of my son Clarence and me when I first heard it by Diana coming off the movie of the same name, which was a favorite as well. As had been the pattern for decades, I did not ignore my R&B past. That's why I included "Hold On, I'm Comin' " and, with a nod to the rockers, the Stones' "You Can't Always Get What You Want." My version of "Hold On, I'm Comin' " wasn't a hit, but it did earn me my eleventh Grammy. I contributed two songs of my own— "Whole Lot of Me" and the title song—and decided to go Hollywood for the cover. I had George Hurrell take the cover shot of me in a chic white linen suit. I wanted my pose to capture the flavor of the Golden Age of Hollywood, the legendary era when Hurrell shot the most glamorous photographs of everyone, including Bette Davis, Ava Gardner, and Joan Crawford.

Around this same time, I initiated the Aretha Franklin Artist Ball, an annual charity event that I sponsored and produced. While it lasted, we had affairs at the Beverly Hilton that featured me, the Whispers, Lulu, and my friends the Four Tops. Money went to causes such as the Sickle Cell Anemia Foundation and the Arthritis Foundation.

In spite of everything, my profile remained high. The Joffrey Ballet put together a program featuring my music. The program toured the world, and, given my love of dance, nothing could have pleased me more. Receiving a star on the Hollywood Walk of Fame was another highlight. Glynn, Carolyn, Glynn's children, and my sons were all there. But when I kneeled down to look at the star, I broke down crying as my dad crossed my mind. I knew how proud Daddy would have been at that moment.

Glynn had personal problems of his own. The week after my father encountered the burglars in Detroit, Glynn's uncle had been shot and killed. We both suffered tremendous losses, and we found our careers moving in different directions. He often worked out of town, as did I. Sometimes we accompanied each other, sometimes we didn't. We couldn't deny the fact that we were moving apart.

# *Jump to It*

~

$T$astes change. Styles come in and out of fashion. Before the jocks start playing you on pop radio—the mainstream stations with big pop audiences in many instances—you have to come through black radio; then you are able to "cross over." Crossing over, of course, is what everyone wants. Crossing over means greater acceptance and megahits.

In the sixties and seventies I had to go through this same ritual. Somewhere in the eighties, though, I finally got to the point where I went on pop radio naturally. I think around "Jump to It" people started dancing and haven't stopped yet.

By 1981 I had released two successful albums for Arista, but I was still looking for that major record, something that would explode with the impact of my earlier smashes on Atlantic. By 1981 disco had started to fade. However, it was fun and I liked some of it. Quincy Jones's initial effort with Michael Jackson—*Off the Wall*—had signaled a return to streamlined productions with soul. That's what I was looking for. When it comes to modern music, I'm always looking, listening to the radio for sounds that catch my ear and touch my heart. With all that in mind, I responded quickly when one day my cousin Brenda asked me if I had heard Luther Vandross. I had. Luther's first hit, "Never Too Much," had caught my ear. He had talent, both as a singer and as a producer.

For a producer interested in keeping classic soul current, Luther seemed the logical choice. When I mentioned his name to Clive Davis, the response was positive. Clive had heard that I, Diana Ross, and Dionne Warwick were three of Luther's main influences. "I'm sure he'll be pleased to work with you," said Clive. And so it happened.

Luther Vandross, man of elegant taste. Big sense of humor. Serious musician, and someone capable of outrageous silliness. I liked Luther and felt fortunate to catch him at the start of what would be his illustrious career. He told me later that he was totally intimidated about working with me, but he didn't let his intimidation get in the way of his judgment. We had a good thing going, a mutual admiration society. We were ready to throw down. Luther and his partner in musical crime, Marcus Miller, turned out a track called "Jump to It" that had all the sugar and spice I required. The groove was extramellow and the message right on time. In the middle I ad-libbed a conversation between me and my friend Kitty in which we deep-dished the 411 on who drop-kicked who. I liked the song because it was contemporary and definitely what you call a summer hit. The song was dynamite and allowed me to be me. "Jump to It" was on the wind and the boom boxes of America.

Luther put together a group of background singers and mixed it hot. Clive revved up his promo crew and, before you knew it, "Jump to It" jumped to the top of the R&B charts, my first number one in seven years. Within weeks it crossed over to pop, and I was feeling like a million. I loved "Jump to It," and it seemed that everyone else did too.

It was logical, then, for Luther to produce the next record. He and Marcus Miller came up with another track I liked, a different groove called "Get It Right." Everything was there, and it was a super follow-up to "Jump to It." I looked forward to the same sort of pleasant experience. I flew from Detroit to New York to cut the record. Then, suddenly, everything went wrong.

All of a sudden Luther wanted to tell me how to sing, when it was I from whom he had learned much about how to sing. My point was simple: If he wanted to tell the artist how to sing, why didn't he sing it himself? His job was to produce and advise the artist about phrasing, diction, and melody, and to be adventurous and say certain things, but definitely not say, "Sing it like this." I definitely didn't need him to tell me how it should be sung. Well, Mr. Vandross wanted to know who had produced my recent number one, and I felt he should be reminded that I had enjoyed at least twenty gold records before I or the world knew his name. I picked up my coat and walked out of the studio as he and I continued shouting at each other.

When I got to the hotel, I called the airport about flying back to Detroit that night. I almost did leave but decided to wait until morning. The next day Clive intervened. Only he could have negotiated the peace. It came down to, "If Luther apologizes, I will too." He did, and I did, although I feel his was halfhearted. We were mature enough to rise to the occasion.

We went back to the studio and finished the song and the album, which, I'm proud to say, included "Givin In," written by my son Clarence. My son Teddy played the guitar on the track. Despite the emotional fireworks between me and Luther, two Aries, our *Get It Right* got it right all the way to number one on the soul charts.

My recording life was back on track, but my personal life was not. I couldn't take the commuting between L.A. and Detroit anymore. It was too much. I felt somewhat unappreciated and taken for granted by Glynn. He understood my feelings and tried to make amends. But it was too little and too late.

Glynn was cool about the divorce. No arguments. After being at home for a year or so, and after long thought, I decided a dissolution of marriage would be the best for all concerned. The prenuptial kept things simple. Glynn moved to a place outside L.A. where his aunt, uncle, and cousins stayed. A little later he started his ranch for underprivileged children. He took me out there to see it, and I was impressed by the good work he was doing. Glynn is a good man. For a while our love burned brightly. When the light faded, it was sad for both of us. But I still consider him a friend and a dedicated artist.

By 1982 it was time to pack up and leave the City of the Angels. I had done what I set out to do—follow the industry and give my best work—but it was far more important to be with Dad.

Our home in Encino held some wonderful memories. Glynn and I had spent happy moments there. My son Eddie was married in our backyard by my dear friend and mentor, the Reverend James Cleveland. Clarence, Teddy, and Kecalf had seen some of the California good life.

Danny Blackwell, the civic leader, gave me a beautiful send-off concert. I was touched to see the artists who took the time to say farewell. Dionne Warwick came, as did Smokey, Gloria Lynne, Deniece Williams, and, yes, Luther Vandross. It was a bittersweet good-bye. I liked the lifestyle, I loved the weather. I would miss my fellow artists and L.A., but I couldn't turn back now.

Detroit. City of my childhood, city of some of my warmest memories and closest friends, city where I learned to sing, city of caring people and my favorite boulevard, West Grand.

I moved back to my father's home on LaSalle. Carolyn and I shared her childhood room, which had antique twin beds. I knew this was where I belonged. Though he couldn't express it, though his condition didn't—and wouldn't—change, I felt my dad was comforted by our presence. Somehow, some way, I felt he knew we were there.

Being in the same bedroom with Carolyn had it pluses and minuses. On the plus side, we united with the common purpose of doing all we could to make Daddy comfortable. On the other side was the question of snoring. Carolyn snored, but she claimed *I* did the snoring. I would call her name each time she started snoring and tell her to turn over. She did, and for a while it would stop. Finally I went as far as to turn on a tape recorder. And the next morning I had proof of who was snoring. We couldn't stop laughing. When we weren't with Daddy upstairs and the nurses, we sat in the living room listening to Martha Jean "the Queen" 's radio gospel hour in the afternoon and often talked to friends stopping by.

This was also a time when Mr. Mystique started calling again. I recall him saying, "You wouldn't marry me," and a few moments passed with me sitting on the side of the bed, only the hall light on and late-night radio playing in the background. I didn't answer, and much later, looking back, I see he was probably right. As long and intimate as they might be, phone calls do not replace the real thing. Mr. Mystique returned to my life later, but right then he was more into himself.

No matter how my family rallied around my father, no matter

how conscientious we all tried to be, we also had to get on with
our lives.

⌒

In the early eighties Detroit was having a bit of a renaissance.
Downtown, for instance, was coming back, nightclubs were popping up here and there, and a young former wife of Henry Ford
opened a chic disco called L'Espirit. The music was good and
throbbing, romantic and moody. They laid on Marvin Gaye's "Got
to Give It Up" or "Sexual Healing," all great music to dance to.
There was an air about L'Espirit that I liked, once you gained entrance.

It was in L'Espirit that my friends Wilbourne and Barbara Kelly
introduced me to their friend and neighbor Chet Trice. Chet had
a polished sophistication and charm I found rather alluring. He
was also fine. We lightly opened up a dialogue that led to his calling and coming over several times. He invited me to a Pistons
game, and, in spite of the appearance of a former friend, we had
a good time, but of course he sweated a little with his former
friend.

Reverend Jesse Jackson came to town for a fund-raiser fashion
show. I asked Chet, among others, to model, and he was fabulous.
The brother had it going on. Prior to all of this I spent an evening
at his apartment. I was taking medicine that didn't allow me to kiss
anyone who had been drinking, and Chet had had a few. We
watched the Grammys on TV, had some easy conversation, and as
we moved toward the door to say good night, he made a move on
me. I had been anticipating his kiss and touch. I was into him to
the max. This could have been and should have been a moment of
mutual desire. But he had been drinking and I was concerned that

the alcohol would clash with my medication, so I regretfully rejected his advance. He was cool and sweet, but I failed to explain to him why I didn't respond in a positive manner. I guess I should have, but I didn't. But the pieces still fell in their proper places. He's married today, and God doesn't make any mistakes.

# Fear of Flying

I'd noticed for some time that flying had made me slightly uncomfortable. When I returned to Detroit after the run-in with Luther Vandross over "Get It Right," for example, I felt small pangs of fear on the plane. Little by little the experience of flying had grown very stressful. Still, I managed. Then one morning in 1983, I got up at 7:00 A.M. to catch a flight to Atlanta. It proved to be a rough day. When we arrived at the office of Mayor Andrew Young, an old friend, no one knew where we were supposed to go or what we were supposed to do. I was to be honored, but the plans were still being developed. Andy was out of town, and we spent hours just waiting for his staff to pull it all together. Afterward, I went straight to the hotel and to bed. The next night I did two shows, and I was reinvigorated but anxious to get home. As a result of signing lots of autographs, I missed my flight. The last thing out was a two-engine prop. I took it. *Big mistake.*

The plane did a couple of those drastic drops, which nearly did me in. We were bouncing all over the sky, and, to say the least, I had an anxiety attack. When I finally put my feet on solid earth, I knew how the pope feels when he arrives somewhere and kisses the ground. I kiddingly told my road manager, Norman Dugger, "You don't have to worry about getting me on another plane soon." However, I didn't feel it would be permanent. All I needed was a little time and I'd start flying again. But that never happened.

I now realize I should have gotten right back into it and taken another flight. I should not have let my fear get the best of me and let so much time go by. But it did. Over the years I've attempted to conquer this fear. I signed up for US Airways' Fearful Flyer program. I took the course. It was a well-planned, step-by-step procedure. We sat at the gate and watched the planes come in and out. Finally, in the last phase of the program, we all sat on the plane as it went down the runway and did what is called an aborted take-off. Before my group was due to take an actual flight, though, I was in concert, so I missed the final two weeks. I decided I wasn't ready. It is my intention, however, to conquer the fear. I flew for twenty-three years, and I will fly again.

My fear of flying has had an impact on my tour scheduling. I haven't been back to California since I left in the early eighties. It's been even longer since I've been in Europe. I have had to turn down hundreds of offers to appear all over the world. Africa, Japan, Egypt, Australia, China are just a few of the places I did not go when I was flying. I understand that in these countries I have large followings of loyal fans whom I would love to meet and see. Generally, I sing in America and travel by custom bus; however, some premier appearances I have been unable to do when asked, for instance, Lena Horne's Kennedy Center Awards ceremony, several fights in Las Vegas and L.A., campaign events in the first and second presidential runs of Reverend Jesse Jackson, the Red Cross Ball in Monte Carlo for Princes Albert and Rainier, a performance for Queen Beatrix of the Netherlands, and so many other wonderful invitations. No matter, I've adjusted. I love my custom bus—lots of R&R, videos, great reading, movies, cooking, and stops for different attractions along the road. New York, Chicago, Atlantic City, Philly, even Miami and New Orleans, are part of my itinerary. But Los Angeles is still a little too far for me. I think about the old days on the gospel trail, with Daddy driving through those narrow mountain passes.

Because of my fear of flying, I was unable to get back to California when my son Clarence, through no fault of his own, was embroiled in an incident that infuriated all of us.

Clarence wanted to stay home for a while, then moved to New York before heading back to Los Angeles. He was visiting friends in our old Encino neighborhood when he decided to take a walk while listening to music on his portable radio. He stopped to rest in the parking lot of a Ralph's supermarket and a woman grew suspicious. I don't know why, other than he was a young black man with a boom box. All reports indicated that Clarence, as always, was perfectly peaceful and minding his own business. The woman called the police, who sped over. They turned Clarence around to handcuff him and, in doing so, yanked his arm all the way up his back. The pain was excruciating. Clarence tried to get the policemen to stop, and they reacted by assaulting him with a billy club and knocking him to the ground. He was bleeding and hit by a female and a male officer. After being abused, he went to jail for thirty days. The police made *him* the problem. I immediately hired an attorney to represent him.

Naturally I was concerned for my son's safety. I asked some of my relatives on my mother's side who lived in the area to visit him regularly. For a while we discussed various ways of dealing with this brutality legally. Finally we decided it was in Clarence's best interest to simply let it go. I understand another very well-known singer's brother was abused in a similar manner, but out of respect for her privacy, I will leave the story for her to tell.

It was late in 1983 when a producer came to Detroit to discuss a Broadway musical about Mahalia Jackson. He wanted me to play the lead. I was interested. I felt I could do justice to Mahalia's character and style of singing, having seen her in our home for years. Besides having been brought up in the gospel world, in which Mahalia was such a leading star, I shared her love of down-home soul cooking. I respected the sincerity of Mahalia's religious convictions and considered her an exemplary Christian. Daddy had the highest respect for her. And, as the world knows, she could stomp-down, flat-footed *sing*. Yes, I said, I'd be honored to play Mahalia.

Broadway appealed to me. Artistically, I could spread my wings there. I signed the contracts and began learning the material, songs like "Didn't It Rain" and "Move on Up a Little Higher." At that point, even though my traumatic flight from Atlanta was still recent, I figured I'd be flying again by play time. I'm an optimist. I was so optimistic that I sent my singers ahead of me to start rehearsals. Those singers were on my payroll, so my commitment was clear. When it came time for me to get on the plane and fly to New York, though, I found I still wasn't ready. We were gonna have to drive.

So we headed for New York on the road. I had forgotten about the rigors of the road and the long distances between cities. After four or five hours, all I could see in front of me was highway. With another fourteen or fifteen hours to go, I didn't think I could make it. It didn't occur to me to break up the drive into two days. So we turned around and headed back. I had to pass on playing Mahalia.

The Broadway producer did not take the news well. I understood. He'd invested a lot of money in the production, and it all revolved around my participation. I had good intentions and genuinely wanted to go ahead, but the drive was too long and the flying too much. To make a long story short, I was sued and had to pay the whopping expenses involved, which my accountants later told me the Internal Revenue Service would not accept as a write-off. No matter, I still hold the artistry of Mahalia Jackson in the highest esteem—and always will.

Nineteen eighty-four was a difficult year.

Jackie Wilson died in January. When I was still a young girl and budding singer, he and Sam Cooke had taken me on the road and protected me like big brothers. Jackie was also like a brother to my brothers, Cecil and Vaughn. Jackie was polished and magnetic and sexy and basically a beautiful man, an entertainer's entertainer. He left nightclubs filled with women screaming for more. Women loved his flash and fire, and men loved his tough-minded stance. Jackie was no pushover. He ran his own show and ran it brilliantly. After his heart attack, he lay in a coma for nine years. When he died the music had moved on, and, sadly, many had forgotten his huge contribution. But I didn't forget, and many others didn't either. I remember Jackie, the music and the man.

Another artist for whom I had enormous respect and love, Marvin Gaye, died in April of the same year. Marvin had been close to our family. He and Erma dated during his early years in Detroit, he and Cecil were good friends, and Marvin and I always enjoyed great camaraderie and warm friendship. I remember seeing him when we went to England in the early eighties. He did not look well. As we pulled up to the Savoy Hotel, he came over to the limo and we got out and embraced. He and Berry Gordy were feuding, and Marvin had quit Motown. Marvin was living in exile in London, and I could see unhappiness written all over his face. But his charm always shone through. I was happy to see him and delighted when "Sexual Healing" brought him back to the country and back on top.

"Sexual Healing" won at the American Music Awards. Marvin walked backstage after winning in his silk, black-on-black-pin-striped custom tux and hugged me, asking, "Do you still love me?" My response was "Absolutely." He was happy, and I was happy for him. There's nothing better than that kind of platonic relationship between friends and fellow artists. Marvin was one of the true Motown geniuses. Because that genius was largely developed in Detroit, we claim him as one of our own. The world loved him as a magnificent singer and composer who could go all the way from "Let's Get It On" to "Wholy Holy." Marvin was about spiritual grace.

Also in 1984 the day we all feared came, and my father passed on July 27. He was sixty-nine. Five long years had passed since he fell into a coma, five years during which his loving family and true friends—Fannie Tyler; Rosalyn Fields; Ms. Edna Harriston, head of the C. L. Franklin Scholarship Fund; Lola King; Deacon Mel Hatcher; Wallace Malone; Reverend S. L. Jones; Reverend O'Neil D. Swanson, Sr.; Reverend Jaspar Williams; Reverend John Webb; Reverend Charles Adams and Reverend Herbert Hinkell; Roby McCoy; Nellis Sanders; Reverend Loyce Lester; and others—stood by his side. Daddy was gone, and his suffering had ceased. As in "The Eagle Stirreth Her Nest," God had opened the door and he had been set free. His soul had taken wings, but his spirit will live forever in our hearts and minds and in the memory banks of thousands throughout the United States and Europe who came out to hear and see him.

The suffering was over. The agonizing decisions that we had

been forced to make were now behind us. At one point we were concerned about the doctors performing a tracheotomy because if they did Daddy might never regain the voice that had brought the message of God to millions. The fact that his sermons are still available, though, means his voice will never be silenced; it will become a permanent part of the religious departments in various colleges.

Exemplifying the Christian spirit and Christian charity for over thirty years every Sunday, as an orator, Daddy had no peer. As a pioneer in broadcasting and recording, he led the way. As an intellect and a human being, he was a giant.

The funeral at New Bethel was difficult. Before we entered the church, there was an argument in the lobby between my sister-in-law and my sister Erma over who would follow whom. It should have been clear from the very beginning to my sister-in-law, who was there by marriage, that the family should be first and it should have been Cecil and Erma who decided who would follow whom. I got so mad I gave one person (who shall remain unnamed) a shove, thinking, *Don't you dare disrespect this service and my father and our last moments with him.* Jesse Jackson stepped between us, I caught myself, and my respect for the church and what was at hand prevailed. Immediately thereafter we entered the sanctuary; my knees buckled, but I managed to stay standing and started down the aisle.

The eulogies were stirring. Pops Staples and Johnnie Taylor and Jackie Verdell were all moving. Reverend Jaspar Williams, his best friend's nephew, did the eulogy. Jesse reminded the church that it was my father who preached his ordination sermon. He said, "C. L. Franklin was a prophet. C. L. Franklin was not just rare but unique; famous because he was well known but great because of his service. C. L. Franklin was born in 1915, fifty years after slavery, and fifty years before we had the right to vote. He was born in poverty, but poverty could not stop him. He was born in segregation. It was illegal for a black man to get an education. No public accommodations, no right to vote, blacks on chain gangs. No friend in the White House, no black member of Congress, no black mayor. Born in poverty. But when God wants a flower to bloom, no drought can stop it. His flower did blossom.

"And so we say thank you for a petal, for an insight, for a sermon. When the eagle stirred its nest, the flower blossomed."

And no, it wasn't just Daddy's deacons or trustees who came out for my father. It was all of the people of Detroit who remembered and respected him and all the good things that he had done for over three decades. I saw people standing on the tops of buildings around the church because they couldn't get inside. The service was played over loudspeakers on the streets. Throngs crowded the neighborhood in every direction as far as you could see. The choir sang like they had never sung before. To the people of Detroit, to those who came from near and far to remember him in the last moments, I and the Franklin family thank you.

# Freeway

After my father passed, I had no desire to move back to Los Angeles or New York. I was home, and of course it was right. I lived in the suburbs outside the city and for a while I also kept a pied-à-terre downtown at the Riverfront Apartments for those times when I needed rest and relaxation and needed to get away from the phones and paperwork. Detroit was—and will always be—my home.

Detroit also has its share of dynamite studios. I liked the idea of recording close to home and, since producers and duet partners were willing to come to Detroit, the city became the center of my recording life. Since 1984 I've cut all my albums in Detroit. They say there's no arguing with success, so I'm not arguing. Detroit has been good to me.

After the little flare-up between me and Luther Vandross during "Get It Right," I realized it was time to find another producer. One of the people whose work impressed me most was the young soul singer Stacy Lattisaw. I liked the productions of her duets with Johnny Gill. I noticed her producer was Narada Michael Walden. When I mentioned his name to Clive Davis, the reaction was positive. "He's a brilliant new talent," Clive said. "I'll arrange a meeting."

You might think it wouldn't work: I'm an Aries, just as Luther is an Aries, just as Clive is an Aries. Narada is an Aries. That's a whole lot of fire. Can all these Aries possibly work together? Absolutely! When professionals are truly professional, even astrological suggestion can't stop the music.

It didn't take long to see that Narada is a gem. He's a happy spirit, a beautiful and gentle human being with his own way of bringing out the best in everyone around him. He's fun and knows exactly how to strike the balance. He writes, arranges, and produces with great vitality and joy. No personality problems, no attitude, no it's-gotta-be-done-my-way-or-the-highway. The moment I met him, I knew we would work together beautifully. What I didn't know, however, was that our first time out we'd create one of the defining hits of my career.

We called the album *Who's Zoomin' Who?* The title was mine, an expression I remembered from my days with Wolf and the New Breeders. They'd say, "This chick or the brother really zoomed me," meaning someone had pulled the wool over their eyes or conned them skillfully. Well, at the time I was dating a gentleman who was actually convinced he was zooming me. He's one of these guys who is a legend in his own mind. The truth was that boyfriend wasn't zooming anyone, and certainly not me. So the question became, Who's zoomin' who?

Narada loved the expression and set it to music. He generously gave me song credit for the title, and we cut it in a flash. Even though I was interested in contemporary material, I also cut—and produced on my own—a song I had recorded twenty years earlier, Van McCoy's exquisite "Sweet Bitter Love." The new string arrangement gave a modern feeling to the timeless melody. When I sang it as a youngster, I knew it was beautiful. But singing it as a mature woman, I more deeply understood and appreciated the lyric. Who can't relate to "Sweet Bitter Love"?

On the cutting edge, we turned to the Eurythmics, who expressed interest in recording with me. Clive and I were delighted that they flew from London to Detroit, where Dave Stewart produced and Annie Lennox sang a duet with me, "Sisters Are Doin' It for Themselves," a song Clive felt was a surefire hit.

Cute story: Annie and I experienced a bit of a role reversal. I got ready for the session by putting together a fun look for myself—a Levi's jacket and a lot of rhinestones. Meanwhile, Annie went to the other extreme of fashion. She turned up in an elegant black pantsuit and the style of spectator shoes I like to wear. I could relate. Anyway, we had a blast and the song rocked—big-time.

The song also meant something. It was my first musical declaration of clear-cut women's liberation. I've always considered myself a progressive woman. And more and more in the eighties, I saw women competing for jobs reserved for men—not just doctors and lawyers but construction workers, traffic cops, FedEx workers. My attitude was, You go, girl, If you've got the heart, do it. And if you do it, you sure deserve the same money a man makes.

For me, integrity is the name of the game. I am a woman of integrity, and "Integrity" was a song I wrote and produced on *Who's Zoomin' Who?* The song challenges the opposite sex; I suggested that a gentleman I was dating look up the word in Webster's dictionary. I believe there would be a lot less problems, and more understanding and happiness, between the sexes if we both applied integrity.

The strongest cut on the album, though, was between my voice and an absolutely upbeat and hot track hooked up by Narada called "Freeway of Love." This was the "Freeway" that would take me all the way on an extended throw-down. "So drop the top, baby," I said, "and let's cruise on into It's Better Than Ever Street." That's the street that took me across the finish line into the winner's circle at the Grammys. "Freeway" was an across-the-board smash, R&B and pop. Everyone related to the magical metaphor of freeway driving; everyone loved how Clarence Clemons (of Bruce Springsteen's E Street Band) greased it up with his grits-and-grind tenor.

"United Together" started the ball rolling at Arista; the George Benson duet kept the ball rolling; "Jump to It" was a major smash; and now "Freeway" was the super crossover I'd been looking for. During the summer of '85, "Freeway of Love" was one of the songs. "Freeway" also introduced me to the world of extravagant videos. The concept was all automotive and all Detroit. I loved it. I showed up in a punk hairstyle. It was time for a change—and the compliments told me I'd made the right move. We shot in Doug's Body Shop in Detroit, a restaurant where the car motif is taken to the max. You eat in booths made from the interiors of vintage autos. In fact, the classic pink Cadillac used in the final scene, where I'm driven off, once belonged to Jayne Mansfield. The name of Jayne's husband, Mickey Hargitay, was written all over the glove compartment. Except for that final scene, which was in color—we needed to see the pink of the pink Caddie—the video was shot in black-and-white to render the feel of the hardworking city of my youth.

Home meant the beautiful woodsy suburbs of Detroit. I lived with Cecil for a year, then I found a small but lovely house on Country Club Drive in Bloomfield Hills, an exclusive section of homes. It was the last house available, and I took it because Kecalf had to start school. After several years I moved to a magnificent home, also in Bloomfield Hills, on Scenic Court, a private cul-de-sac. With enormous trees and green fields, it was like living in the country. The house itself was contemporary, a dramatic split-level design featuring a sunken living room that overlooked the back-yard.

I enjoyed the pool and especially the vegetable garden. I proved to have something of a green thumb and cultivated a variety of herbs and the largest squash you've ever seen. I began to see the virtues of the stay-at-home woman Roseanne refers to as a "do-mestic goddess," but I have always loved my home. I enjoyed phone calls to close friends or an afternoon spent reading a good book. I like biographies, being a people person, and I love just groovin' with my man. Life doesn't have to be hectic to be exciting.

It was a summer day when the breeze off the river downtown cooled me from the hot sun. My buddy Stormin' Norm Dugger and I were walking along the street facing Riverfront Apartments when I noticed a man sunning in the grass. I couldn't help but ob-serve that he was tall and handsome and had a beautiful body. He asked us to join him. One of us said, "Now why would we just join him?" and we walked on. Then I heard him call my name. "Please sign my cast," he asked. Well, okay. He was a fireman named Willie Wilkerson, who had broken his leg after jumping off a fire truck. I admire firemen, civil servants who display great courage in the line of duty—who, in fact, risk their lives for us all. And this fireman, I must admit, was kind of cute. Turned out he also lived in Riverfront; he lived in the west tower and I lived in the east. That made things rather convenient—and interesting.

Lightly and slightly, we started seeing each other. I think I saw things in Willie others may have missed. He was basically a kind and good man with a sharp wit. There was a part of Willie that was mischievous, and sometimes he liked playing the bad boy. He loved music, especially the Whispers, and so did I. You could say that the songs of the Whispers provided the background for our blooming romance. We boogied at the L'Espirit, and dined at the 1940 Chop House, an elegant, upscale restaurant out on Jefferson that Emanuel Stewart, boxing trainer, purchased later on. Before you knew it, we had begun to date. Willie turned out to be a wonderful escort.

I like a man who can cook something, and Willie was mean in the kitchen. We'd have a ball in the midnight hour when he'd fry up those steak-and-onions meals just like they cook in the fire-house. And you know those secret barbecue recipes that men won't give you? Well, Will had a few of those.

When our schedules coincided, he accompanied me to some out-of-town appearances. I recall once in Chicago when we were walking down the steps of the Drake Hotel. A young lady suddenly approached Will. Apparently she was a former friend, and I got the impression they had been close. That was confirmed when she asked Will if she could see him later, and all this was said in my presence, in low tones but loud enough to hear. So who did she think I was—his Chicago tour guide? "Don't you see I'm with someone?" Willie said, and with that he and I walked on, leaving that girlfriend standing there.

Boyfriend passed the test with flying colors. The more Willie traveled with me, though, the more women were coming out of the woodwork. Some older women started calling him and asking him to meet them at different places, like at the health club or restaurants, boldly propositioning him. Willie had a way with women and, to his credit, he handled it very well. He showed me respect and let these women know, as he had done so capably in Chicago, that he was no longer a hot commodity on the open market.

# I'm Pressing On

After the roaring success of "Freeway," I zoomed back into the studio with Narada Michael Walden and got to work on the follow-up album, which we called simply *Aretha*. I asked Clive Davis to commission a cover portrait by Andy Warhol—I loved it—and the hits kept coming.

The biggest hit off the record was "I Knew You Were Waiting (for Me)," a duet with George Michael, who enjoyed such success with Wham! George was a pleasure. He came to Detroit with a wonderful attitude of eager cooperation, so that made two of us. The song went all the way to number one pop. It became the biggest duet of my career—and still is.

Another couple of hip Englishmen, who played with a little band called the Rolling Stones, also came to Detroit. Keith Richards wanted to produce me doing his "Jumpin' Jack Flash" and brought the guitarist Ron Wood along to lend a helping hand. Keith and Ron were really cool. Keith wanted me to play piano, and I hadn't done that in a long time. I also loved the idea that the song would be included in Whoopi Goldberg's movie *Jumpin' Jack Flash.* As a matter of fact, Whoopi herself came out to Detroit to shoot the video with me and the Stones. She played one of the background singers. I decided to dress for the occasion. But how does a lady dress for a video with the Stones? How 'bout tiger-striped tights, superbad black leather jacket, and a purple punked-up hairdo with a funky ponytail hanging to the side?

On the more conservative side, I went back to my roots and sang and produced a song I heard as a child by Dinah Washington, "Look to the Rainbow." I also produced the self-penned "He'll Come Along." As I wrote in the liner notes, "Many thanks to myself for being disciplined and growing as a producer. I'm absolutely delighted with my productions."

The new wave of success was very satisfying. But it made me reflect: by the time the summer of 1987 rolled around, it had been fifteen years since I had gone to Los Angeles for *Amazing Grace,* and my dad had been gone for three years.

Ever since *Amazing Grace,* fans have never stopped asking me to make another gospel record. It was always in the back of my mind to do just that. Now it was time. I wanted to honor the cherished memory of my father, just as I wanted to feel the excitement, strength, spirit, and inspiration that come only in church. I decided that no matter how well my pop records were selling, I owed it to myself and my fans to honor tradition. I regretted that it had been so long since *Amazing Grace.* I felt moved to renew the original musical faith in which I was born.

Clive Davis was most agreeable. He understood the artistic and spiritual validity of the project and entrusted me as its one and only producer. My plans were simple: do a gospel album, just as we did *Amazing Grace,* as a religious service. Record in New Bethel, located on Linwood, now renamed C. L. Franklin Boulevard by Mayor Coleman A. Young. Enlist the help of my sisters and brother. Invite the best gospel artists in the country. Solicit the participation of the ministers I enjoyed the most. And select the songs closest to my heart.

I'm delighted to say that it happened as planned. As I stated in the notes of the album I called *One Lord, One Faith, One Baptism*, it was "truly a pièce de résistance of gospel."

When I think of those three magical nights in August, what stands out most is that we had a shouting good time and that old and new friends worshipped together and praised His name. I had invited Mavis Staples, and she and Yvonne, her sister, drove over from Chicago. Carolyn, Erma, cousin Brenda, and I were singing together for the first time in a very long time. Big Mama, confined to a wheelchair, was also with us. We didn't know the difficulties that would soon follow; we couldn't see the tragedies around the bend. But for those three nights we were together as a family, singing and praying as we did as children. The spirits of our mom and dad were surely with us.

I wanted to hear and see a service like the ones I saw as a child, a candlelight service when the choir walks down the aisle of the dark church, only the flickering flames illuminating their way. I wanted to hear and sing the songs that had moved me when I was barely old enough to walk. I wanted to go all the way back to my roots.

To hear the prayer invocation by my brother, the Reverend Cecil Franklin, was extremely moving. As you might imagine, Cecil had some of the inflection and cadences of Daddy. But Cecil was his own man, with his own preaching style. It was also appropriate to have the Reverend Jesse Jackson introduce my sisters, my cousin Brenda, and me. We had come a long way together. Jesse introduced me as "Sister Beloved, the one who wears the coat of many colors."

With my sisters behind me, I sang two songs associated with Clara and the world-famous Ward Singers—"Jesus Hears Every Prayer" and "Surely He Is Able." Both songs I'd loved as a little girl, fondly recalling the moments in the lobby of the Church of Our Prayer when I had my first chicken-eating lesson with Clara Ward. It was also as a young girl that I had met Mavis Staples. From the pulpit I reminisced about how our families met on that dark Mississippi road back in the days when I was traveling with my dad. Then we rang out with "Oh Happy Day," the great gospel classic by the Edwin Hawkins Singers, followed by "We Need Power." Between me and Mavis, though, there was no lack of vocal power.

I'm sorry to say that subsequently Mavis made negative statements about me to the press. I was disappointed, to say the least, especially since I remembered her and supported her when she needed a friend. True friends don't diss each other to the media or otherwise. I tried to help Mavis when she was down and talking about quitting, and was disappointed to read her untrue comments about me in *Elle* magazine, as I had invited her to come to Detroit and be a part of my gospel LP project. I heard through reliable sources she felt played down in the final mix on our duet, so I guess she felt justified in her statements. Well, I *didn't* play her down, but I sure didn't feel like she should be louder than I was on my album. Mavis has a very *heavy* voice, and for us to sound equal, I had to put her just below me in the mix. Perhaps Mavis and I can mend the fence on a more mutually respectful basis. It's up to her. I sincerely hope she can rise to the occasion as a woman. But that night in New Bethel we sang as sisters and old friends.

It was a particular joy to include the Reverends Donald Parsons and Jaspar Williams. Both men were admirers of my dad. Long live the whooping style of preaching! I loved it when Reverend Williams started shouting, "I'm pressing on!" while I sang in between his words, just as I had done with my dad. "Sometimes you have no one to call but Jesus," said the preacher. "Just plant my feet on higher ground."

"Higher," said Reverend Williams.

"Higher," I sang back to him.

"Higher," he repeated.

"Higher," I echoed.

"Oh, higher."

"Yes, higher."

"Higher ground!"

The rest of the service was magnificent. The New Bethel choir joined the choir of Thomas A. Whitfield. The sensational singing of Joe Ligons of the Mighty Clouds of Joy, dueting with me on "I've Been in the Storm Too Long," led to an altar call when we opened the doors of the church and invited worshippers to come home and be candidates for baptism. People came. People jumped and shouted during the thunderous finale with Mavis, Joe, my sisters, and me as we brought the message home, talking about the New Jerusalem, with Clara Ward's "Packing Up, Getting Ready to Go."

*One Lord, One Faith, One Baptism* was received with great enthusiasm. I was honored when the album won two Grammys, one for me for Best Female Soul Gospel Performance, and another for Reverend Jesse Jackson's spoken-word contribution to it. But more than the commercial success, the camaraderie and service did my heart good. Gospel is and will always be an integral part of who

I am. Gospel is the good news—His birth, His life, His resurrection. Gospel is all feeling and faith and about the life and teachings and miracles and trials and prophecies of Jesus, a music of unshakable conviction and determination that things will get better. Its root is rock-solid optimism and the certain knowledge that God is real.

I've said it before and I'll say it again: I am a traditionalist when it comes to gospel, and it doesn't mean I don't appreciate the modern forms. There are many ways to praise the Lord. Different generations hear different beats. I must say, though, that when the bass lines are pure boogie and the beats are pure funk, I wouldn't call it gospel. And when it makes you want to dance and pop your fingers, believe me, it isn't gospel. When the performer's body language is funking so hard as to be religiously disrespectful, then I wouldn't call it gospel. Gospel is a higher calling; gospel is about God. Gospel is about beautiful and glorious voices and spirit-filled performances and people who are anointed. When it comes to God's music, men like Joe Ligons and James Cleveland and Claude Jeter have some of the voices I like best. I need that old-fashioned, stick-to-your-ribs gospel, the kind that will carry you as far as you need to go. As Dr. King used to say after a dynamite dinner, "I can go around the world on a meal like that." Well, I can go around the world on the best gospel.

In the world of secular music, I was gratified to be called a pioneer of rock and roll. I say that because in 1987 I was selected as the first woman to enter the Rock and Roll Hall of Fame. It came at a time when I had stopped flying and long drives were also out of the question, so I didn't attend the ceremony. But I was honored nonetheless. Earlier inductees included Ray Charles, Sam Cooke, and James Brown. Along with me the Hall of Fame admitted Bo

Diddley, Marvin Gaye, and B. B. King. Good company. A few years later, when they opened the Rock and Roll Hall of Fame and Museum in Cleveland, Ohio, largely due to Ahmet Ertegun, chairman of Atlantic Records, I drove down there, performed, and was happy to see myself enshrined in this magnificent institution on the lake.

Now getting back to Willie: He was a good friend. He stood by my side during the making of my gospel album, accompanying me through my long hours in the mixing studio. He also began to travel and assist me on the road. That proved to be a mixed blessing. I certainly appreciated the help, but I didn't appreciate the one instance when he criticized me in the press.

The story is that I had performed with the Boston Symphony. Upon leaving town on the bus, I discovered my music had been left in the venue. We had to go back and get it. Any artist in this business can tell you that musical arrangements are very expensive. And in talking to a journalist, Willie made me look like a temperamental witch (please rhyme this word), adding that he was no pissing post. Well, neither was I. And it's not cool to dis a friend, and more than that, it's especially uncool to dis your woman to the press or anyone else. I expect certain things from some people but was shocked to read he had actually said these things.

In the late eighties, the pressures on me, which had to do with the welfare of my brother and baby sister, were growing intense. Within a period of two years, the two of them would suffer in ways I could not have imagined. Will was there for me during those tough times. But there were other things that were not cool. Out of respect for his and my privacy, I won't discuss it. We simply agreed to disagree. However, Will's wit was in rare form as he helped me chase away the blues after those many treks to see Carolyn and Cecil in the hospital. I'll always be grateful to Will for helping me through the storm, as I supported him when his mother passed. The end of our relationship was easy, cool, and respectful. We remain good friends today.

# Through the Storm

It was the name of my last album of the eighties, but *Through the Storm* also described what my family was going through during that time. The storm was stronger than I could have expected; it took a tremendous toll. Before I deal with the difficulty of describing what happened to my loved ones, though, I'd like to tell you about the record.

After my gospel album, it was time to do a secular record. I brought back Arif Mardin, who had been producing me for over twenty years, and Narada Michael Walden. The first song was with the Godfather of Soul himself, James Brown. I've always liked James. At a very important point in the history of our music and the civil rights movement, James Brown came in and did his thing in Detroit, calming the black community over the radio after the assassination of Dr. Martin Luther King. Musically, James set the pace for all the funk that followed. James had the grooves and James had the moves. Like Jackie Wilson, he was the consummate soul entertainer. For historical reasons, I thought a duet with James would be appropriate. It was called "Gimme Your Love."

Under Clive Davis's guidance, Cissy's daughter Whitney Houston, whom I used to call Nippy and met as a little girl, was fast developing into a star. Because we were labelmates, and because she intimated in *Jet* and *Ebony* that I had inspired and influenced her, everyone thought a duet with Whitney was a good idea. As it went down, some things were misunderstood and we miscommunicated; we were very badly mismatched in terms of maturity and experience and sensitivity. It was something that never should have happened. I think Nippy felt unappreciated, and nothing could have been further from the truth. But the song, "It Ain't Never Gonna Be," turned out well, and I continue to appreciate her and sincerely wish her the best. I'm still her Aunt Ree, and she can come to me for support or advice anytime.

I've enjoyed a lifelong love affair with the Four Tops, my buddies from the good old days. Their lead singer Levi Stubbs is in a class of his own. He has wiped me out with renditions of "MacArthur Park," "Bernadette," and "Still Waters Run Deep." We partieeeeeeed. So I was thrilled to sing "If Ever a Love There Was" with them. Kenny G's solo was the cherry on top of the cake.

I have always liked Elton John and noted his musical expertise. So when Clive suggested we sing together, I quickly agreed. The song, Diane Warren's "Through the Storm," was so strong it became the album title.

The Elton–Aretha duet made some noise, but nothing else on the record really took off. I was disappointed. Artists have peaks and valleys, though, and I've been in the business long enough to know to go with the flow. No artist can produce a hit album every time out. If I was going into a quiet period, I could accept it. I had other, far more pressing matters on my mind.

Cancer is a frightening word and a frightening disease; cancer struck two of my siblings, Carolyn and Cecil, within a period of two years. In both cases the disease proved virulent. I am grateful that I had the opportunity to be with my sister and brother during their last months. I was in awe of their strength of character and the battle that each waged.

The first indication of medical problems with Carolyn had come while she was living with me in Los Angeles. Standing at my front gate, which had been closed by remote control, she rang the bell, but no one was there. She tried to squeeze through where some of the bars were slightly bent from an old mishap and broke the skin on her breast, which caught on something on the fence. She required treatment, but there was no indication of anything serious. After she moved back to Detroit, though, those initial indications and diagnoses proved wrong.

Carolyn and I were staying together, and I knew she had gone to see the doctor. When she came back and I opened the door, she rushed past me and ran upstairs to her room. I immediately felt something was wrong, but I decided I would wait for her to come downstairs to talk to her. In the meantime I asked my cousin Brenda to come over. Later I learned that one doctor had been especially brutal. He said he didn't understand how she was still alive. The next day Carolyn and I went down to Riverfront, where I encouraged and advised her the best I could, suggesting she see our gynecologist, who would refer her to a specialist. After a biopsy, though, the diagnosis of breast cancer proved accurate. Carolyn started going for outpatient radiation treatment, and for a while she responded very well.

Carolyn spoke to Big Mama. She wanted to be sure our grandmother knew that, as the Franklin family matriarch, she was cherished and respected.

"Where are you going?" Big Mama asked Carolyn. "You sound like you're going away." Carolyn didn't explain.

The cancer had set in, proving more aggressive than we originally thought. Carolyn had problems walking and trouble talking. I hired licensed practical nurses round the clock, as I had done with my father. Carolyn picked one of those nurses, Miss Ruth Edwards, who had cared for Daddy. Everyone loved Miss Edwards. Carolyn moved into my home on Scenic Drive.

I am sorry to say that my sister Erma and I didn't always see eye to eye, although for the most part we did. I asked her, for example, to spend the night at my house so I could have the evening off and go into the city. She refused, saying that her nine-to-five job was all she could handle. Erma kept saying how she needed to sleep in her own bed. She was working at a home for wayward children, doing evaluations. I didn't know what it was like to have the daily grind of a nine to five. I knew she was tired—we all were—but I was also pissed at her reluctance to pitch in that evening.

During the ordeal, it was Carolyn who inspired us. She was working for her degree at Marygrove College in Detroit, and, cancer or no cancer, she was determined to graduate. Despite the enormous pain, she kept up with her studies and completed her required courses. When she was in the hospital, her good friend Beverly Bradley brought her silk pillow slips and Erma brought nightgowns and necessary articles, and we all alternated staying with Carolyn regularly.

At one point Carolyn was given a clean bill of health and her doctor said they saw no signs of cancer. We rejoiced and felt she would make it. Then one day, after she began running a temperature, she learned an infection had set in and the cancer had spread.

The fever meant she couldn't receive radiation, and valuable time was lost. Carolyn was in and out of the hospital a number of times. We would talk daily when she felt good, and I would visit the hospital regularly. I recall leaving one night and looking up and waving to Carolyn in the window. I could see only her silhouette and small frame as she waved back to me. I felt so sad and unsure. We were all praying for Carolyn.

When graduation came, she was extremely weak and unable to walk. I catered her graduation party. We put Carolyn's cap and gown on her, and she received her degree in bed. It was a proud but hurting moment for all of us. I stood against the wall, fighting back the tears. I was so upset with the people at the college and refused to interact with them. They had sought to deny Carolyn's degree while graduating another student who had cancer as well, making things as easy as possible for the other young lady. I had no time for these people. So instead I concentrated on helping my sister relish the day. We brought her chair into the living room, and for a short while she was able to enjoy the company and the great honor being bestowed upon her.

Carolyn died on April 25, 1988, a little over a year after her cancer had been diagnosed. For all the pain of her passing, I knew in my heart that she was at peace. She loved the Lord, and she had lived a life filled with generosity and caring, giving creativity. Carolyn's spirit will never die. She lives on in the beauty of her songs—"Angel," "Ain't No Way," "Ain't Nobody (Gonna Turn Me Around)"—and her songs, like the love she gave so freely, ensure her immortality. I think of her in so many ways all the time.

Cecil died December 26, 1989. The cause was lung cancer. I first learned about his illness when Cecil called and told me he was coming over; he had something very important to tell me. At first he said Dr. Young thought he might have TB, but he was waiting for his test. He and his wife, Earline, rang the bell, and it was in the foyer where he said it was worse than he thought. It was cancer. But he was going to do everything he could to beat it. I was stunned but continued to talk to him in the positive. There was little time to recover from losing Carolyn before we learned that Cecil had cancer. It was sudden and shocking.

I remember Cecil accompanying me to Washington, where I received an honor from the United States Senate. By then he had to carry oxygen. But he didn't have to use the oxygen outside the hotel. As we left the award presentation in the Senate chambers, I realized I was walking too fast for him. I slowed down immediately. In slowing down, I really realized I had to remember he wasn't quite as strong as his usual self. He was so courageous, and he held his head high and walked every step of the way like the true champion he was. A true lesson in courage, faith, and determination. We were hoping for the best and all praying for Cecil.

At that time I had established the Aretha Franklin Scholarship Awards. Each year we'd have a lavish banquet. Proceeds went to deserving minority students in the Detroit area who lacked the financial means to attend college. But more about that later. I was appearing at the Masonic Temple. Dorothy Donegan, whom my father had brought me to see at the Gotham Hotel when I was a child, entertained. Dorothy still had it. So did the soul singer Peabo Bryson and the Four Tops. Cecil was having a hard time that night, so he and Earline came just a little after me, but he came nevertheless. He found the strength to show up, to smile, to rally around the cause, and to be the big brother I could always count on.

Later on he was in and out of the hospital, and Smokey Robinson came and prayed with us. Smokey was Cecil's closest and best friend ever since they were small boys.

And the memory remains: I was in my apartment at the Riverfront when out of the darkness I heard Ruthie Bowen's voice come over the answering service. It was about 2:00 in the morning. "Aretha," she said, "get to the hospital." The tone in her voice said it all. I knew it was going to be rough and I would need some support, so I called Beverly Bradley, who lived in the same complex. She got dressed and came over immediately. It was wintertime and it was cold, and I remember trying to put on a pink jumpsuit. All I had to do was zip it up and belt it, but it seemed like it took me forever to put on that jumpsuit. It kept coming out the wrong way, and I kept hearing Ruthie's voice: "Aretha, get to the hospital."

On the way over there was silence in the car. All of a sudden I just broke down. By the time we arrived at the hospital, Cecil was gone. Erma and Earline met me at the front door. I kept asking where was Cecil, where was Cecil, but they wouldn't answer, trying to get me to the family waiting room before saying anything. I tried to go in and see him but couldn't. We were all crying. Erma was there for me. She helped me, and we walked to another part of the hospital.

Like those of my father and sister before him, Cecil's funeral was held at New Bethel, where, years earlier, he had served as Daddy's assistant pastor. He certainly had the capacity to be a world-renowned preacher. Cecil was my greatest friend and greatest fan in addition to being my brother. I admired and loved him greatly. He was a brilliant man. *Ebony* once wrote that he was "my greatest asset." Amen. No other manager, no other person, no other loving spirit could ever replace him.

We had barely caught our breath when, in 1990, we lost Big Mama. Ever since she had fallen out of bed and broken her hip, she had been living in a nursing home. While there, she had cataract surgery, which seemed to work wonders. After she came out of surgery you could hear Big Mama up and down the halls testifying. "Thank you, Jesus!" she was shouting for days. "Thank you, Jesus!" she said. "It's not about the going in, it's about the coming out of morning surgery." She also loved to sit in front of the TV and yell at *Mannix;* she loved telling him how to solve his cases.

Big Mama died peacefully, a wonderful and great woman who had seen her son grow from a sharecropper to an international figure. She supported Daddy with loyalty and undying strength. And she supported me—in fact, she supported all her grandchildren and great-grandchildren—with the same steadfastness. She was a person of tremendous humor, and I'll always remember her little dance and the funny expression that went with it. Mostly, though, I'll remember her faith. Her faith sustained her all the way. Big Mama's faith was the backbone of the Franklin family.

# Stormin' Norm's Back

When my road manager, Norman Dugger, returned, I was over-joyed. Just before he left, we had clashed slightly. It was our only bad moment in twenty years. I had been short with Norman, and he didn't respond well. He decided he would go home to his family and, because of health problems, take it easy. Later he wrote a long, appreciative letter to me. Norman knew how much I'd need a friend after my brother was gone, so he returned and stayed several years. It was great having the company of my dearest and truest friends. Norm stayed until he retired to his Virginia home, where he opened a restaurant with his brother.

My brother Vaughn was a twenty-five-year serviceman, a navigator in the Air Force and exemplary human being. He has five children and was living with his second wife in Alabama when I called to see if he could travel with me and road-manage. Absolutely, of course he could. Vaughn has proven to be a blessing, someone who's organized, honest, and dependable. He takes care of business and is a lot of fun to boot.

Speaking of family members, let's talk about cousin Brenda. Brenda has a beautiful soprano voice, is of strong character, and can be extremely charming when she wants to be. But as one of my singers, Brenda felt she didn't have to comply with certain rules of the group. We had guidelines that we all had to respect, and when I would speak to Brenda, she would often respond in an unprofessional manner. After twenty-three or twenty-four years of traveling and singing with me, she told a local newspaper that she had quit because it took me too long to pay her. Would you call being paid before she had even sung a note on most occasions too long to pay her? Brenda's my cuz, I love her, and we both know—and everyone else in the group, particularly the singers, knows—that that wasn't the truth.

Brenda, Margaret Branch, and Sandra Richardson were my main singers. I always relate to and have fun with and treat my singers and musicians and anyone who works for me very well. After all, I'm a singer myself. Sometimes I cook for them on the tour bus, and other times I'll hire cooks to cater fabulous meals. After special performances, many times I buy small gifts as mementos of the occasion, and their salaries are more than commensurate with the best in the business.

I've come to the conclusion that there can be as much rivalry among cousins as there is among siblings. I've had a change of heart about asking relatives to work with me unless they are mature people like my brothers, Cecil and Vaughn, who take their responsibilities seriously and don't play games, are not insecure, and don't have ego problems.

I look back at two incidents with my sisters with similar regrets. Both happened when they were interviewed on television specials about me. After Daddy died Carolyn told a journalist, on camera, that all the family was worried about whether I'd survive his death. I couldn't believe the implication. As I watched her, my mouth fell open. Had she forgotten about my faith and trust in God? Had she forgotten about the strength of character I exhibited all my life? In truth, we were all raised by the same father, who instilled within us the spiritual strength to survive the most trying times.

Erma made a similar statement, telling an interviewer that I was a shy person who only came alive onstage. She said I was an introvert, the biggest lie ever told about me. I am as sociable an extrovert as anyone, and my very profession demands that I meet and interact with thousands of people all the time. As a child I was somewhat shy, but as an adult I could hardly be called introverted. For nearly twenty years I talked and interacted with people all over the world, and I did so quite easily and comfortably on and off the stage, as well as talking to the press nationwide. For nearly twenty years I have given the most fabulous parties in the city. No one loves a party more than I; as I have said, I am a people person. When people are introverted, they may be unable to reach out and enjoy other people. They may suffer through their inhibitions and be deprived socially, which is the exact opposite of who I demonstrate myself to be on a daily basis.

The irony is that Erma, not I, can stay at home for months on end. Getting her out of the house is a major chore. "I have nothing to wear," she'll say, or come up with some other excuse. One of the rare times I succeeded was taking her to a Nancy Wilson concert. Like Nancy, Erma is a Pisces, and as a result of my pushing her to get out more, Erma is blossoming socially and professionally, meeting new supporters and friends at my parties.

Erma certainly wanted to have a career of her own. And she was good. Very good—a formidable vocalist. She worked hard for her success. After she came off the road with Lloyd Price, though, her career became dormant. And when she put no further effort into it and decided she was through, that closed the book on it. I remember her exact words when she came to terms with that fact: "Aretha," she said, "it don't scare me none to get a job." She did get a job, and since then has always held good positions in organizations geared to help children in need. I respect that highly. However, it seems to me that Erma—not I—was in retreat after 5:00 P.M.

Hopefully, there is no resentment. I realize, of course, that my career may not always have been easy on my sisters and cousin. Yet they have reaped far more benefits than hardships, and dealing with my success should have required minimal coping skills *if* there was a problem. They will never have a better sister or cousin, and we all know that.

I want to emphasize that Erma has many beautiful and endearing qualities. She took charge of our dad's estate and, as guardian, has done a superlative job of keeping his papers in order and honoring his legacy. I admire all of her efforts on his behalf. And Erma is basically a very good, caring, and compassionate person.

But when it comes to unjustly criticizing me in public, let's stop the B.S. We're grown, mature, and responsible women. We've been through a lot together, shoulder to shoulder, the painful deaths of a mother, father, brother, sister, and grandmother. Life is going to hand us all some heartache and things beyond our control. Let's not contribute to it by disrespecting each other. I have worked very hard for thirty years and feel I have earned whatever success I have. And I am grateful and thankful for it and loyal fans and friends, and I would certainly never apologize to anyone for it.

Mr. Mystique reappeared on the set in the eighties. This was the same charming gentleman who had fascinated me previously, just touching base to say hello and all was well.

My emotional investment in this man was increasing, and I began to ask myself, Was a real and meaningful and growing relationship with him possible? Then things started going left. It began as a simple request one evening after a day of bantering back and forth about some firewood with my son. I thought Mr. Mystique might be the right person to speak to him. Coming from a man, I thought a few words of wisdom and direction might be appropriate. But when I asked him to speak with my son, he was short, curt, and edgy. Damn near rude. His attitude was, What is it? I'm really busy, you know, but I'll do you a favor. I decided he would have been the absolute worst person for my son to talk to. It was becoming clear that he was a take-all kind of person, who would give as little as possible or just enough to be decent and keep up a front. It made me wonder whether he ever really cared for me at all. I dropped it, but I was so disappointed.

Sometime later Mr. Mystique was in a bind and needed some money. He had gone to friends, but they wouldn't help. I said I would, but it would take me a little while to put the money together, be patient. But patience was not one of Mr. Mystique's virtues. He called on a Monday to ask about the loan. Not yet, I said. Then he called on Tuesday and Wednesday, and every day, until he really began to get on my nerves. There's a little red tape involved, and this is going to take some time, I said. His impatience during this episode was another warning; another facet of his personality that I had never noticed before was beginning to flare. Maybe he wasn't the man I imagined him to be.

You could call it the telephone relationship of a lifetime. When it was good it was very good. But when it came crashing down in the nineties, there was no way to build it back up. Mr. Mystique turned out to be Mr. Selfish, Mr. Self-Centered, Mr. Self-Serving, and Mr. Full of It.

I went through a couple of other scenes before Mr. Mystique played himself out. He flew to Detroit and spent a couple of hours with me. We had lunch, we were warm, but part of him remained distant—distancing was the name of the game at that point—and he was still playing a role. Afterward, we were all hugged up in the back of the limo on the way to the airport. He asked to look at my ring. It crossed my mind, *Was he considering replacing it with a wedding ring?* Or he'd do things like hum Mendelssohn's "Wedding March." And of course the suggestion was there. We promised to stay in touch.

But months passed without my hearing from him. Finally, I found out where he was staying and called his hotel. By then I was good and pissed. He heard my attitude and tried reverse psychology, putting me on the defensive. He implied he would call me when he was good and ready—and on his terms, not mine. I couldn't believe he was in this groove. My respect for him was diminishing. Minute by minute, call by call, my romantic notions were diminishing, and, of course, it was all part of his plan.

Flash forward to a major music festival down South. I had just performed and was walking offstage when I picked him up in my peripheral vision. He was standing in the wings, with an intense gaze on his face. The hell with him. I walked past him without saying a word, walked straight into my dressing room and shut the door behind me. I changed clothes, refreshed myself, and left to speak with friends. I saw Mr. Mystique walking toward me. He stopped just short of me, and when I didn't acknowledge his presence, he walked past me. I was tempted to turn in his direction, but I didn't dare. I was still too much in love with him and would have run into his arms. However, I avoided his gaze and continued talking to friends as the words *Be still my foolish heart* echoed in between our chatter. My pride prevailed.

Sometime later I was performing in New York when, before the show, a bellman brought an exotic bouquet of flowers with a note saying, "You'll always be in my heart." For a while our dialogue resumed. His charms were still contagious, and he was as smooth as a pickpocket who never rings the bell set to catch him. And just like the pickpocket, he had stolen my heart.

Here was a man, I finally concluded, who segued from passionate conversations and love to major B.S. in a matter of days. Here was a man who led me on knowing he wouldn't deliver, a man who wanted nothing to do with emotional involvement. I perfectly understood that I was neither the man's wife nor his woman. Mr. Mystique was a major player. He spoke out of both sides of his mouth and finally couldn't be believed on any level. It took me a long time to see how my naïveté was blinding. But once I did see clearly, I realized there was nothing more to say. The less I thought about him, the better. Now I rarely think of him at all.

❧

At the start of the nineties, after Cecil passed, I went looking for a new business representative. I chose to speak to each candidate myself. I was amazed how rude and egotistical these big names could be. When one well-known figure in the industry came to the phone the second day after receiving my contract for him to sign, he barked, "Yeah, what is it?" in a tone I couldn't believe. They had been all peaches and cream the day before. "Sorry," I said. "I must have the wrong number," and hung up.

Luther Vandross was back on the scene in 1991, when I did an album called *What You See Is What You Sweat.* We did a duet on a cute Luther tune called "Doctor's Orders." As I said before, Luther can be a very charming person, and because he produced the song, he was in charge of the mix. And therein lay the problem. He had my voice so far down in the mix I sounded like one of the background singers. Naturally I complained. Loudly. "No, no, no," I said, "this is not how this song is going to be mixed or released." Once again Luther and I were crossing swords.

I wanted an impartial producer to do the mix, someone without prejudice and someone who was not singing on the song. But Luther didn't go for it. He didn't want anyone else mixing his song. He put the word out so strongly that other producers were reluctant to interfere. Finally we got a remix out of Luther that was acceptable. But the feelings between me and Mr. Vandross were strained.

A few years later, when Luther came through Detroit on tour, he called me, and during the course of our conversation, I invited him to dinner at Opus One, one of the best restaurants in the country. It was a great evening. Luther brought me a delicate hugs-and-kisses friendship pin from Tiffany; he has so much class on occasion. On the way to my house he insisted around midnight that we stop at Blockbuster and get Eddie Murphy's *The Nutty Professor.* Luther had seen it and said I'd love it. He was right; it was a scream.

The next night was Luther's concert. I went with my friends Lisolee and Ron. Luther had invited us to his dressing room before the show. We arrived, but he wasn't there. We waited for nearly a half hour, but when Luther didn't show, we decided to walk around the lobby and see some friends. So we left a message for Luther. When the show was over—Luther's shows are always extravagantly entertaining—I went back to his dressing room and complimented him on his performance. But being the sensitive artist that he is, he had an attitude because we had left earlier. Anyway, all the good feelings from the night before—the scrumptious meal with him, the pin from Tiffany, the hilarious Eddie Murphy movie—were gone. Maintaining an even relationship with Luther has proven to be more than a notion sometimes. However, he's still fabulous and a likable person, and we're cool even when we're not.

*What You See Is What You Sweat* was not a hit album, but it did contain some gems. "Ever Changing Times" was written and produced by Burt Bacharach and Carole Bayer Sager and featured Michael McDonald shadowing me on the chorus. The title song was the contribution of Pic Conley, a red-hot producer in the early nineties. I brought Narada Michael Walden back to update the Sly Stone classic "Everyday People." I wrote and produced "You Can't Take Me for Granted," which includes guitar work by my son Teddy. I also wrote "What Did You Give," including an introduction in French. To keep the French flavor, I asked the great Michel Legrand to produce the song.

In 1992 I was not dominating the charts the way I had in the late sixties, but I was still hitting, and I was not unhappy with my releases and was right in the middle of the mix. Then my career was suddenly boosted by an unexpected source: presidential politics. The Democrats were back in power.

# Hail to the Chief

⌒

And with the coming of President Bill Clinton, my career hit a new and even higher plateau. You never know what the Lord has in store for you.

It was great to know that both the president and Hillary were Aretha fans. They explained that they grew up on "Respect." The president let everyone know that he loves straight-up soul. To have a fellow baby boomer—and a bubba and a saxophonist to boot—in the White House, well, let the party begin.

The first big party was Clinton's 1993 inauguration. I performed at two inaugural balls and on the inaugural telecast. I wore a violet-tulle-and-silver Bob Mackie evening gown with an evening scarf. They were glamorous events, closing it all out with Fleetwood Mac doing their signature song, "Don't Stop Thinking About Tomorrow." My colleagues that evening were Fleetwood Mac, the Alvin Ailey Dance Theater, Barbra Streisand, Barry Manilow, and many others. I received some criticism because of the sable coat I was wearing; I was not aware of the animal rights activists and the fur controversy. In fact, I recall asking Dionne Warwick that evening, as cold as it was, why she wasn't wearing her fur. Singers and speakers, because of perspiring and the pores being open, are more susceptible in cold weather to pleurisy, bronchitis, and pneumonia. Dionne had no real response to me; she just smiled.

I have sparkling memories of singing in the Rose Garden at the White House after the emperor and empress of Japan had been received there; I was joined by my longtime buddies Lou Rawls and Les McCann. Billy Kyles came up from Memphis to bear witness that evening as well, and Ron and Alma Brown, and so many others.

In 1994 I was the youngest artist to receive a Kennedy Center Honor. My escort was Renauld White of New York, high-fashion model extraordinaire. We went to the East Room of the White House for the opening statement and ceremonies, after which we were accompanied to the presidential box, where soft drinks, tiny demi cups of tea and coffee, and finger sandwiches were graciously served. I was surrounded by my fellow honorees—the actor Kirk Douglas, the composer Morton Gould, the director Harold Prince, and the folk singer Pete Seeger. In attendance was also an interesting Saudi Arabian prince. Now the beautiful thing about the Kennedy Center Honors is that, rather than have to entertain, you are entertained by your peers. You just sit there and enjoy it all without having to exert a muscle. I was pleased when Patti LaBelle performed in my honor and called me her "hero." Patti is a very animated diva and on the real side to say the least. The Four Tops also sang.

Each of my visits to the White House has been exquisite with one exception: the evening I met another musical diva whom I will have the good taste not to name and who is an artist of exceptional gifts. I was delighted to meet her. But because of an innocuous statement I made about her escort, she became just short of irate, and tempers began to flare in harsh tones under one of the great works of art in one of the historic rooms. My good manners and upbringing prevailed. However, I couldn't have guaranteed that had we been outside about a block away from the White House. But as we sashayed away from each other, our parting gesture was the finger. I was really disappointed to learn that the private woman did not measure up to the public artist.

Nineteen ninety-four was my fourteenth year with Arista. I was happy to mark the occasion with a *Greatest Hits* of my Arista-only material. I was pleased to note that since 1960 I had been with only three labels. And I had enough hits for three separate *Greatest Hits* collections. With my Arista compilation, though, I wanted something more than past hits; I wanted new hits. And thanks to Kenneth "Babyface" Edmonds and David Cole, I got more than my wish: I recorded two very hot records.

Clive Davis, whose unerring instincts always sought out new talent, had established a business relationship with Babyface early on. And when Clive brought me the Babyface ballad "Willing to Forgive," I knew it was right. Along with Daryl Simmons, Face wrote and produced it; the result was a major smash. The lyrics reflected a story that, in one way or another, I would tell in several songs in recent years: "I'm willing to forgive you," I sang, "but I can't forget." The story of a man who isn't what he seems is a story that I—and, for that matter, millions of women—can easily relate to.

The second fresh song on the Arista *Greatest Hits* was "A Deeper Love," a sizzling club mix that hit the top of the dance charts. The kick-up-the-heels track and lyrics came from C+C Music Factory's David Cole and Robert Clivilles, whose "Gonna Make You Sweat" had burned up the discos. "A Deeper Love" got extra play when it was put on the soundtrack of Whoopi Goldberg's *Sister Act 2: Back in the Habit.*

The same year that Arista's *Greatest Hits* appeared, the Grammys said I had done and was doing something right by honoring me with their highest award: the Lifetime Achievement. Carlton Northern, one of my longtime hairstylists, had cut and raised my hair, and, as my makeup artists say, "My face was beat." I really felt like a queen. When I received the award, my sons Teddy and Eddie stood immediately behind me, and in the excitement of it all I forgot to introduce them. I was doing all right in my speech until I got to my brother Cecil; I just couldn't hold back the tears. The illustrious Danny Glover presented me with the award. (I just couldn't stand his character in *A Raisin in the Sun,* which shows you what a terrific actor he really is.)

Back in Detroit I continued the Aretha Franklin Scholarship Awards dinners, an annual event. The artists came to Detroit— Chaka Khan, Oleta Adams, the Four Tops, Tevin Campbell, Eartha Kitt—to support the scholarships for young honorees from the community. I performed as well. Eartha was especially fabulous. She swished over to my dressing room with a drop-dead black beaded-and-tulle gown and did a little mini fashion show with a few pivots and turns here and there. That night Detroit fully appreciated Eartha. The Franklin Awards have become one of the major events of Detroit's social season.

Occasionally, I would read reports in this paper or that paper about how I had become a recluse. Recluse? Please. I was concertizing from one end of the country to the other, doing TV specials, recordings, and everything else that artists do. I love giving fabulous affairs, sometimes in my backyard and sometimes in downtown hotels, where TV monitors run some of my favorite movies, like *Dr. Zhivago,* on an endless loop. I've given luaus and fish fries. I've had entertainers at those affairs ranging from Sinbad to Tito Puente, the Gap Band and the Ohio Players to Angela Bofill and Temptation Ali "Ollie" Woodson, Wilson Pickett, Bobby "Blue" Bland, Johnnie Taylor, Nnenna Freelon, and so many others. Annually I throw a Christmas party as well. During the summer I love to barbecue. Guests include friends from the past as well as new friends and people I have loved and cherished for a lifetime.

Since my brother passed, I've had to take charge of my own finances. That has not always been easy. In the late eighties a certified check for eighty thousand dollars made out to me was never found. This threw off my money matters, and I began to fall behind with the IRS. Unfortunately, I was never apprised of the true situation, and it took years to remedy the situation and find new business representatives.

It irks me that celebrities are sitting targets for this sort of negative publicity and our privacy is sometimes invaded terribly. However, for the most part the press has been absolutely fabulous with me, and I love them, love them, love them, love them. The truth is that I'm a highly responsible person and have many accounts in Detroit and, for that matter, all over the country with businesses who value, respect, and appreciate my patronage.

Last year I gave three glorious concerts with the Detroit Symphony Orchestra, and the support was tremendous. On New Year's Eve I sang at the Sinai and Ford Hospitals, which the patients and

I enjoyed very much. Detroiters realize how deeply I appreciate the city in which I was raised, and it is in Detroit that I continue to cultivate my career; it is to Detroit that I direct most of my charitable activities; and it is from Detroit that I receive much love and support, which I reciprocate.

# Aretha Is Still Aretha

⸺

And "A Rose Is Still a Rose." That's the name of the song that Lauryn Hill of the Fugees penned for me. Clive Davis and I were the catalysts. Lauryn came to Detroit and brought her adorable infant son, Zion, along with her mom, who helped with the baby. Lauryn directed the video as well. She's a young woman who knows what she wants; she's responsible and long on patience. I've read that a couple of critics were comparing Lauryn with me. Where do these people come from? She and I are as different as night and day. But we have a common denominator, being positive sisters striving to give our best. I thank her a mill for a "A Rose Is Still a Rose" and wish her the best. I'm always here to advise her if necessary.

The song itself speaks to women, stressing that self-esteem is not dependent on anything else but you and service to others. A rose is and will always be a rose. Nothing and no one can ever take that from you. The song is about inner beauty, women understanding that the deepest validation comes from God.

Clive and I liked the song so much it became the title of my latest album. And the public liked it so much it became a major crossover hit, big on the R&B charts and a pop smash as well. At the time of this writing it has turned gold and is on the way to platinum. To have an across-the-board hit at the end of the nineties, nearly forty years after my career began, is a source of tremendous satisfaction.

I was really down with these productions of Sean "Puffy" Combs, Jermaine Dupri, Dallas Austin, and Lauryn—not to mention veterans like Narada Michael Walden. It was also great to see that the critics were as enthusiastic about *Rose* as I was. Mainly I thank my fans and audiences for their longtime support—it is golden. I thank all of the program directors, the jocks, the one-stop people, the Arista group and former Arista personnel—my home girl Audry LaCade, Tracy Jordan, Jerry Griffith, Richard Smith, Roy Lott, Donny Einer, Gwen Quinn, Michelle Mena, Ken Levy, Jennifer Helpern, and Barbara Shelley.

I've been called a diva, queen diva, diva supreme, and I love it. However, that's really for others to decide, not me. But I do accept it as the ultracompliment, and it was hard not to feel like a diva when Ken Erlich gave me my own duets TV special, with guests Rod Stewart, Elton John, Smokey Robinson, Bonnie Raitt, Gloria Estefan, Robert De Niro, and Dustin Hoffman.

When VH1 asked me to appear on their "Divas Live" program with Gloria Estefan, Mariah Carey, Celine Dion, and Shania Twain, I was delighted to oblige. VH1 has been loving to me over the years, and I've always enjoyed their programming. The New York audience could not have been more enthusiastic, and Clive Davis and Donald Trump were there that night. It was a particular pleasure to end the evening on a gospel note with an old-fashioned, down-home, romping and stomping gospel rendition of "I've Got a Testimony."

I've thought a lot about divas. They are fabulous. But everyone who sings or has a hit record is not a diva, in my opinion. Real divas are ladies like Sarah Vaughan, Ella Fitzgerald, Judy Garland, Grace Bumbry, Lena Horne, Shirley Bassey, Patti LaBelle, Renee Fleming, and others whom I'm sure I'm forgetting but of course they know who they are. There are other divas who carry off the diva persona but are not as well known as some of the names I have mentioned: Clara Ward, my original inspiration; Dinah Washington was an absolute diva; Shirley Caesar, a gospel diva—although I am sure that Shirley Caesar sees herself in more humble terms as a servant of God. Josephine Baker was a supreme diva. Divas are great fun. Everyone loves grandiosity and a larger-than-life personality.

I must admit that on the night of the fortieth annual Grammy Awards at Radio City Music Hall I certainly felt like a diva. Earlier that week, at the MusiCares dinner at the Waldorf-Astoria, I had been asked to sing for Luciano Pavarotti. My selection was his signature number, "Nessun dorma," the beautiful and haunting aria from Puccini's *Turandot.* Afterward, Mr. Pavarotti embraced me exuberantly. Later I learned he was in great pain and was due for hip surgery. Before the evening was over, though, he invited me to his home in Modena to sing with him. He promised me he would send his private jet and fly with me from point to point in Italy. I'm still considering the generous offer.

That was on a Monday. On Wednesday I sang "Respect" on the Grammy telecast. I had recently sung the song in the film *Blues Brothers 2000,* and the live performance, with Dan Aykroyd and his fellow Blues Brothers, was geared to promote the new film. Afterward, I was in my dressing room preparing to leave when the producers ran in. Pavarotti was just not well enough to sing "Nessun dorma," scheduled about fifteen minutes from then. Would I have total recall of the aria? I thought about it for a few seconds before saying, "Absolutely, yes."

What followed was chaos. People began looking for a boom box backstage while I sat quietly. People were chatting as I tried to concentrate on the tape of the aria being played. I realized that this orchestration was much grander than the one I had sung on Monday. It was also written in Pavarotti's key, not mine. There was no time for adjustments or modifications. And certainly no time for rehearsal. This was do or die. Someone was kind enough to remind me that 1.5 billion people throughout the world would be watching.

I did it. I sang the aria, and the ovation from my peers was wonderful. I sang Puccini because I love Puccini. It was God who gave me the gift of song, and it is God who keeps me strong in that gift.

Some warned that opera purists would go after me. That was the least of my concerns. The next day people in the streets of New York were smiling and waving and saying the most wonderful things about my performance. Critics say and believe this opened a new genre of music for me. I certainly hope so. I have been gratified to receive many invitations from national symphony orchestras. In the past they requested I sing my popular songs with them; now they want classical material as well, the arias. Ever since I heard my sisters practicing their classical pieces on piano, I have been drawn to these melodies. They have always been in the background of my life. I have felt capable of singing classical material in my own way. And I recall the days when our home was the happiest and all was well, and there was classical piano in the air, someone—Erma or Carolyn—rehearsing. The point that pleases me most is that, in singing Puccini, I am able to keep the integrity of my own interpretation.

No matter how far I may venture into other genres, my heart remains in soul and the soul of my people. I think of the past and many of my soul music colleagues. Some are gone, some are singing better than ever. It bothers me that the artists of my generation are being shut out by radio programmers. The public still wants to hear these singers. But the jocks and program directors seem to be so youth-oriented that many veteran artists are not getting on. I wish the system was more equitable.

⁓

I have dreams for the future.

In the immediate future I will enroll at Juilliard and take those courses I mentioned earlier. I want to improve my skills on piano. I realize that I have not given nearly as much time to the piano as I can. And I can play piano a lot better; I have just focused more on my voice.

I have my own production company and record label under the banner of Crown Productions and World Class Records. So far I have recorded a magnificent Christmas gospel concert at New Bethel (with me) and have recorded with artists like the Jackson Southernaires, Rudy Stanfield & Choir, Albertina Walker, and Stephanie Mills in Carnegie Hall. I also plan to cut an album of classical arias. I will lessen my concert schedule to allow time for my legitimate business interests, my grandchildren, my music lessons, and my man—and not necessarily in that order.

Moreover, Detroit is on the verge of another renaissance. Three new and glamorous casinos are being built, and hopefully Aretha's Chicken and Waffle restaurants will be part of the mix.

I will never stop dreaming of returning to Europe. Africa appeals to me. I want to see Egypt and I want to see Israel, but I especially yearn to visit Paris again and enjoy the Ritz or the Plaza-Athénée cooking school. I've been to Europe four times to date, and I look forward to the Champs-Élysées and the City of Lights again.

Look for my first cookbook, *Switching in the Kitchen with Ree,* soul cuisine at its very best. And, speaking of eating, I'm still battling the additional pounds I put on since I stopped smoking. It has been the hardest thing I've ever had to accomplish. I work out, run, jog . . . but it's just no good if I can't do it at least three times weekly. Having to leave for concerts disrupts my diet because my scheduling on the road is vastly different from my schedule at home. But I will find a way to make it work.

God has been so good to me; my life has been and is rewarding, exciting, and creative. And surely the best is yet to come. There are many songs that I want to sing.

And sing . . .

And sing . . .

And sing . . .

And sing . . .

And sing . . .

And sing . . .

And sing . . .

# Selected Discography

The following albums are currently available
on either cassette or compact disc:

## Universal Music

You Grow Closer *(Peacock Gospel Classics)*

## Columbia

Sweet Bitter Love

The Great Aretha Franklin: The First 12 Sides

Aretha Sings the Blues

Jazz to Soul *(Legacy)*

Unforgettable: A Tribute to Dinah Washington *(Legacy)*

The Early Years *(Legacy)*

The Great Aretha Franklin/Sweet Bitter Love/Aretha Sings
   the Blues *(Legacy)*

This Is Jazz, Volume 34

## Atlantic (reissued by Rhino)

Aretha Arrives

I Never Loved a Man (the Way I Love You)

Aretha Now

Lady Soul

Aretha in Paris

Soul '69

This Girl's in Love with You

Spirit in the Dark

Live at Fillmore West

Young, Gifted and Black

Amazing Grace

Hey Now Hey (The Other Side of the Sky)

Let Me in Your Life

Sparkle

Aretha's Jazz

30 Greatest Hits

Queen of Soul: The Atlantic Recordings *(4-CD box set)*

The Very Best of Aretha Franklin, Volume 1: The 60s

The Very Best of Aretha Franklin, Volume 2: The 70s

Love Songs

The Delta Meets Detroit: Aretha's Blues

## Arista

Love All the Hurt Away

Jump to It

Get It Right

Who's Zoomin' Who?

Aretha

One Lord, One Faith, One Baptism

What You See Is What You Sweat

Greatest Hits (1980–94)

A Rose Is Still a Rose

# About the Authors

ARETHA FRANKLIN has won more Grammys—fifteen—than any female in history and was granted the Lifetime Achievement Grammy Award. The first woman to be inducted into the Rock and Roll Hall of Fame, she was also the youngest recipient of a Kennedy Center Honor. The state of Michigan has proclaimed her voice a natural resource. Miss Franklin lives in Detroit.

DAVID RITZ, a three-time winner of the Ralph Gleason Music Book Award, is the best-selling biographer of Ray Charles, Marvin Gaye, B. B. King, Smokey Robinson, Etta James, Jerry Wexler, and Sinbad. His novels include *Blue Notes Under a Green Felt Hat;* his lyrics include "Sexual Healing." Mr. Ritz, who won a 1992 Grammy for Best Album Notes, lives in Los Angeles.